CENTRE FOR EDUCATIONAL RESEARCH AND INNOVATION

School: a Matter of Choice

ORGANISATION FOR ECONOMIC CO-OPERATION AND DEVELOPMENT

ORGANISATION FOR ECONOMIC CO-OPERATION AND DEVELOPMENT

Pursuant to Article 1 of the Convention signed in Paris on 14th December 1960, and which came into force on 30th September 1961, the Organisation for Economic Co-operation and Development (OECD) shall promote policies designed:

- to achieve the highest sustainable economic growth and employment and a rising standard of living in Member countries, while maintaining financial stability, and thus to contribute to the development of the world economy;
- to contribute to sound economic expansion in Member as well as non-member countries in the process of economic development; and
- to contribute to the expansion of world trade on a multilateral, non-discriminatory basis in accordance with international obligations.

The original Member countries of the OECD are Austria, Belgium, Canada, Denmark, France, Germany, Greece, Iceland, Ireland, Italy, Luxembourg, the Netherlands, Norway, Portugal, Spain, Sweden, Switzerland, Turkey, the United Kingdom and the United States. The following countries became Members subsequently through accession at the dates indicated hereafter: Japan (28th April 1964), Finland (28th January 1969), Australia (7th June 1971) and New Zealand (29th May 1973). The Commission of the European Communities takes part in the work of the OECD (Article 13 of the OECD Convention).

The Centre for Educational Research and Innovation was created in June 1968 by the Council of the Organisation for Economic Co-operation and Development.

The main objectives of the Centre are as follows:

- *to promote and support the development of research activities in education and undertake such research activities where appropriate;*
- *to promote and support pilot experiments with a view to introducing and testing innovations in the educational system;*
- *to promote the development of co-operation between Member countries in the field of educational research and innovation.*

The Centre functions within the Organisation for Economic Co-operation and Development in accordance with the decisions of the Council of the Organisation, under the authority of the Secretary-General. It is supervised by a Governing Board composed of one national expert in its field of competence from each of the countries participating in its programme of work.

Publié en français sous le titre :
L'ÉCOLE : UNE AFFAIRE DE CHOIX

© OECD 1994
Applications for permission to reproduce or translate all or part of this publication should be made to:
Head of Publications Service, OECD
2, rue André-Pascal, 75775 PARIS CEDEX 16, France

Foreword

Measures to improve parent and pupil choice of school have recently become an important issue for educational reform in a number of OECD countries. School choice has been a controversial topic, tied up with ideological beliefs about the nature of public education and the applicability of "market" principles to publicly funded institutions. The debate has not always been based on a clear understanding of what is meant by school choice, still less on well researched assessments of its impact when introduced in various forms in different countries. This study reports on the experience of school choice in selected OECD countries, at a time when evidence of a number of policies introduced in the late 1980s is starting to emerge. While more systematic studies are clearly needed, it is hoped that a better-informed debate will result from the information and ideas that are examined here.

The study is the first in the CERI series under the general heading "What Works in Innovation". These studies are being carried out under a methodology of quick, direct information-gathering led by the Secretariat, followed by reports that combine description of recent practices with general analysis. The approach is described further immediately after the Summary below. The report is intended to help policy-makers and practitioners to understand more clearly how school choice is being interpreted and applied.

The report was prepared by Donald Hirsch of the CERI Secretariat. It is published on the responsibility of the Secretary-General of the OECD.

Contents

Summary 7

Methodology and structure of the report 8

Part I
THEMATIC DISCUSSION

1. Policies for school choice: objectives, objections and characteristics 11
2. The process of choosing schools: patterns, constraints and policy influences 21
3. The impact of choice 33
4. Choice and the cultural context 43
5. Conclusion and recommendations: aligning choice policies with educational objectives 49

Part II
COUNTRY SUMMARIES

Australia:	Twenty years of subsidy for private schools	55
England:	Creating a public-sector market for schools	61
Netherlands:	Equal treatment for public and private schools	67
New Zealand:	Choice through school autonomy	73
Sweden:	A dose of competition in a decentralising system	79
United States:	In search of an acceptable choice	85

Part III
SIXTEEN CASE STUDIES

Examples of markets

1. Haarlem *(Netherlands)* 93
2. Bradford *(England)* 99

3. Kent *(England)* 103
4. Stockholm *(Sweden)* 109
5. Melbourne *(Australia)* 111

Examples of policies:

To diversify supply

6. Specialised schools in New South Wales *(Australia)* 115
7. City technology colleges *(England)* 119
8. A "profile" school in Helsingborg *(Sweden)*.......................... 123
9. Every school a magnet in Montclair, New Jersey *(United States)* 125
10. *New Zealand*'s support for Maori schools 129

Other policy examples

11. Boston's universal form of public enrolment choice *(United States)*............. 133
12. *France*'s limited experiment in public enrolment choice 137
13. Minnesota: public-sector challenges to school district monopolies *(United States)* ... 141
14. *Denmark*'s "free" schools – liberal support for private education 145
15. Milwaukee's vouchers – limited support for private education *(United States)*...... 149
16. *New Zealand*'s educational development initiatives: community-wide choice 153

Notes 157

Summary

Greater choice of school by parents and pupils is changing the balance of power in education, away from "producers" and towards "consumers". This tendency varies in degree and form in different OECD countries, but is related in particular to two widespread influences. One is a new market-oriented view of educational provision. The other is the "choosiness" of a growing number of parents and pupils, who wish to make their own judgements about the desirability of attending a given school, rather than simply accept the one assigned.

This report looks at policy approaches to school choice, particularly in Australia, England (United Kingdom), the Netherlands, New Zealand, Sweden and the United States. In some cases, rules for choosing a public school have been liberalised, with resources following pupils; in others, subsidies to private schools have been introduced or maintained. In both cases, public schools that once had a "captive" clientele are being subjected to greater competition.

There is no direct evidence that this competition improves school performance. Studies show that parents and children rarely choose schools on the basis of well-informed comparisons of educational quality. However, the dynamic of competing for pupils typically enhances some school characteristics associated with effectiveness, such as strong leadership and sense of mission. Moreover, choice that increases consumer satisfaction can be seen as desirable not only for its own sake, but also because parents and children who support a school help to make it more effective.

In practice, though, the main impact of choice has been on things other than school effectiveness. Choice potentially makes it hard to pursue certain kinds of system-wide education policies, especially those associated with provision of one kind of secondary school for all pupils. There is strong evidence in a number of countries that choice can increase social segregation. Sometimes this is because more privileged groups are more active in choosing "desired" schools. Sometimes it is because such schools are in more prosperous neighbourhoods, whose residents continue to get privileged access to them once they are full. Crucially, a new "choice" of school does not work well in cases where a high proportion of choices cannot be met, because of a concentration of preferences on a few schools with limited capacity.

There are several ways in which these fundamental difficulties might be addressed by policy-makers. Giving popular schools capital resources to expand is an option that has not been much used while overall school rolls have been falling. But it might be used more in the late 1990s, when rolls will rise in most countries. Unequal opportunities in choosing popular schools may be addressed by policies that offer disadvantaged groups more information, more help with transport and possibly privileged access to certain schools.

But ultimately the only way in which more choices can be satisfied is if preferences are more evenly spread. Schools that differ by pedagogical style or subject balance are more likely to be chosen evenly than if they differ by social or academic status. Demand pressures are rarely enough on their own to create such diversity. Initiatives to diversify educational supply may therefore be needed to create a genuine set of choices. Under a uniform model of schooling, choice is more likely to reinforce educational hierarchies than to improve educational opportunities or overall quality.

Methodology and structure of the report

This study was carried out on the basis of information assembled by the OECD/ CERI Secretariat during 1993. In addition to the collection of existing written information, the enquiry consisted of three phases. In January, a preliminary interactive exchange of information by electronic mail between the Secretariat and six country experts (listed in note 1) established a common framework for reporting country experiences, based on a preliminary overview of relevant developments in each country. The experts then produced background papers within this framework, by April. In May and June, a member of the Secretariat visited each of the six countries for a week-long study visit, interviewing policy-makers, researchers, practitioners and other interested parties, at both national and local levels. The report was drafted in July and August, and presented to the CERI Governing Board in November 1993.

The first part of this report discusses school choice thematically, with reference to developments in various OECD countries, but particularly the six included in the study. Part II considers the particularities of each of the six countries. Part III looks at 16 specific cases of school choice in practice, either in terms of the functioning of a local school "market" or in terms of a particular policy aiming to increase choice at national, regional or local level.

The report is intended as an overview of developments rather than a detailed survey of the progress of policies in each of the countries covered. The country summaries in Part II aim to describe the national context that makes school choice in each country different. Greater detail on nation-specific information can be found in the country background papers[1].

The case studies in Part III illustrate various specific aspects of choice. They include examples from all six countries, and also from France and Denmark. The first five cases look at how choices are made and at how schools compete in specific areas covered by local education authorities, and in smaller districts within them. Choice in each of these areas is affected by the context of national and local policies, but also by social, geographical and other factors specific to the local environment. The next five examples illustrate policies to widen the range of options among which parents and pupils might choose, by increasing the diversity of schools. Of the remaining six examples, three describe policies to open up choice of schools in the public sector, two look at subsidies for private schools, and one at initiatives to make choice a matter for whole communities rather than individual consumers.

Part I
THEMATIC DISCUSSION

Chapter 1

Policies for School Choice: Objectives, Objections and Characteristics

This report looks at policies to give parents and children greater choice over which school a child attends. The choosing of a school can have important implications for an individual child, and is often an emotional or self-defining moment for a parent. But in recent years, school choice has also become a matter of critical importance for entire schooling systems. The reason is that in a number of countries, choice has been seen as a means of giving the "consumers" of education greater influence over what goes on in schools, as an alternative to running them entirely according to the judgements of professional administrators and educators. In short, the balance of power in education could be drastically changed by making schools compete for the custom of their pupils.

The report looks in particular at policies in six countries where school choice has been a significant issue: Australia, England,[2] the Netherlands, New Zealand, Sweden and the United States. It also makes reference to other countries.

The notion of school choice is nothing new. But it has traditionally been associated mainly with the freedom of individuals to opt out of an otherwise coercive (compulsory) public education system, rather than to use their market power to influence it. The idea that universal public schooling would threaten liberty caused John Stuart Mill to warn in 1859 that "an education established and controlled by the State should only exist, if it exists at all, as one among many competing experiments".[3] Using that criterion, Mill would have been disappointed by the publicly-dominated school systems that subsequently emerged in most developed countries. But nowhere is the coercion complete: in no OECD country is a child compelled by law to attend a public school. Private schools and, in some countries, schooling at home, are recognised as alternatives provided they deliver an education considered valid by the State.

The degree of choice that was built into education systems after schooling became compulsory depended largely on issues of conscience and on the relationship between Church and State. In countries like France and the Netherlands, where there were conflicts between an expanding State and certain church interests, the compromise was to have heavily-subsidised religious schools alongside religiously neutral public ones. In the United Kingdom, where church schools could integrate relatively easily into the State system, and in the United States, where public support for a religion is constitutionally excluded, private schools have had no systematic State help. In most countries (the Netherlands is an exception), such choice as exists as an alternative to public schools has been available mainly to those willing and able to pay a private school fee (albeit sometimes a very low one), or to educate their children at home.

In recent years, the issue of school choice has again been raised in many countries, but largely in a new context, on which this report concentrates. The central issue is no longer the relationship between a monolithic or coercive State and individual freedom of conscience. Rather, it is the relationship between individuals as clients of an education system and schools as "providers". This is part of a more general concern that developed during the 1980s that public services should become more responsive to their consumers. In the case of education, it is proposed in particular that public schools, just like private ones, should have to attract pupils through choice rather than simply having them assigned. This potentially creates a radical shift in power over schooling. Schools that have been controlled primarily by the decisions of educators, politicians and administrative planners may have to gear their behaviour more directly to the wishes of their "customers".

This report addresses the implications of such changes in the customer-supplier relationship at the school level. But it should be borne in mind that this is part of a wider change that affects all levels of education and training. Education has to some extent been regarded as something that is simply handed down to citizens by benevolent governments or institutions; training as something "provided" to workers by enlightened employers. The growing tendency of citizens and workers to formulate their own demands and to plan their own learning pathways is increased by the notion of learning as an investment, with tangible benefits to the individual. Another important influence is the coincidence of a strengthening of the case for continued learning beyond the school level with fiscal constraints that prevent governments from fully funding it. This implies greater personal investment in lifelong education and training, and hence an enhanced role of the consumer in educational decision-making.[4]

Objectives

There are many overlapping motives for giving parents and pupils a greater role in education by allowing them to choose more freely among schools. In particular, there have been two primary influences, one political and one social, that have affected the policy debate.

The political influence is the neo-liberal approach that has affected public policy-making in a number of countries since the 1980s. In its crude form, this approach advocates a reliance on free markets rather than public planning to manage publicly financed services. In education, this means making schools dependent for their resources on the decision by "customers" to attend them. The idea is that this will create pressure for schools to perform well, and in the interests of their clients rather than (supposedly) of professional educators or administrators. Taken to its extreme, this would blur the distinction between public and private schools, as every school would become eligible for a payment by the State for each pupil that chose it.

The idea of making the market the driving discipline of education has been advocated in particular by American theorists, as far apart chronologically as Milton Friedman[5] in 1962, and Chubb and Moe[6] in 1990. It is interesting to note that whereas no country, least of all the United States, has come close to implementing such ideas in their pure form, the language of the market has entered the education debate and influenced educational policy-making, to varying degrees, in a wide range of OECD countries.

But the concept of consumers choosing their education stems not just from political ideas but also from new social realities. In particular, greater social and geographical mobility and a growing average educational level of parents has changed the way in which schools are regarded. Education is viewed by an increasing number of people as a route to social and economic success, and finding the right school is often seen by parents as a way of giving their children a good start in life. In a consumer-conscious country like the United States, such choices are made, regardless of public policies, by those who are able to move to areas where schools are good or to buy into the private sector. But the desire to choose one's school is not growing only in countries where consumers are powerful, where a high proportion of public schools are seen as unsatisfactory or where private schools are generally considered a superior alternative. In France, none of these conditions apply, yet in the view of a leading sociologist:

"From the lower secondary level upwards, the institution of the school has transformed in the minds of its users into a service-providing organisation... Rather than working for the transformation of schools, the great majority of users accept them as they are, on condition that they are allowed to choose the best on offer".[7]

A further influence, which has not been as fundamental as political and social factors to the emergence of a debate about school choice but is potentially central to its development, is the notion of educational variety. Since the 1960s there has been considerable interest, among sections of the public as well as among professionals, in alternative educational styles. There has also been disillusionment in some quarters with the notion of homogeneous public schools providing a uniform education to all. A degree of diversity and specialisation is seen as a potential means of motivating students at risk of failure, as well as helping to restore a sense of school identity, which is strongly associated with school effectiveness. So the idea of increasing the variety of schools from which parents and pupils might choose is complementary to that of giving them the right of choice.

From these influences, the following main objectives of school choice can be distinguished:
- to respond to an increased desire to choose among existing schools, extending to everybody opportunities hitherto available only to those with the financial means to buy either private education or housing near good schools;
- to create a new discipline encouraging schools to perform well: schools that acquire a good reputation will get more "customers" and more resources;
- to give the values of parents a new place in determining school behaviour: the values of professional educators are not necessarily shared by parents;
- to extend the range of educational choices available: in the past, a number of countries have supported pluralism in schooling by subsidising private religious schools; choice might also support educational pluralism, potentially in the public as well as the private sector.

Although these objectives overlap, differences in emphasis on each of them creates policies with different characteristics. One crucial distinction is between measures designed primarily to use consumer pressures as an instrument for change and those that directly encourage schools to offer new kinds of education from among which to choose. The first can be labelled "demand-led" or "competitive" choice policies: their direct aim is to encourage competition. Typically, they include the introduction of a right to enrol in any school within the public sector, and the establishment of a direct link between the flow of money for public and/or private schools and their enrolment levels. The second kind of measure can be called "supply-led" or "pluralistic" choice policies: their direct aim is to increase the range of schools available to choose from. Support for private schools aimed mainly at allowing religious or educational difference can be included in this policy, as can the encouragement of special-character schools within the public sector, including magnet and other subject-specialised schools.

This distinction between competition and pluralism is a central theme in this report, for several reasons. First, policy-makers are not always clear when presenting choice policies whether and how they expect a greater range of choices to emerge. Second, competitive pressures alone seem rarely to lead to much greater variety, especially among public schools, which see their "markets" as covering geographical areas rather than people with subject or pedagogical preferences. Third, competitive choice tends to create frustration when it is not accompanied by pluralistic choice, for the following reason. Competitive choice relies on consumers valuing the performance of some schools rather than others. Where all schools are aiming for roughly the same results, consumers tend to choose in similar ways. The highest-valued schools quickly become full, leading to disappointment for those who are turned away. The alternative model, of a range of preferences matched by a variety of school types, is a happier ideal, but more rarely fulfilled.

Objections

The issue of school choice has produced controversy and rancour, not just at the political and policy-making level but in local schools, communities and homes. It has provoked emotions by on the one hand appearing to offer an alternative to parents or pupils who are frustrated with their local school, and on the other appearing to threaten the very system of public neighbourhood schooling that many parents support. When discussing choice policies, therefore, the fears and objections as well as the objectives associated with school choice must be taken into account. Broadly, there are four types of objection:

- *that choice might be a fine idea, but it will not work in practice*

There are two particularly strong obstacles identified by critics of school choice. The first is that groups that have always been more privileged educationally will do most of the choosing. The same people that might potentially choose good schools by selecting their place of residence or paying for private education may also be best placed to take advantage of extra choices theoretically open to all. They may have better access to information and to transport, and broader horizons.

The second potential obstacle is the problem referred to at the end of the previous section: of popular schools filling up, and choices quickly being closed off. This raises questions about how schools in "open" enrolment systems select their pupils when they do not have space for all applicants. Such a situation may arise where, as is often the case, a government allows recurrent resources but not capital resources automatically to follow pupils. So popular schools are not allowed to expand, or unpopular ones to fail: unlike in a pure market, supply does not adjust to match demand.

- *that choice might work, but it will have undesirable side-effects*

Some critics claim that any benefits of choice will be outweighed by negative consequences, intended or otherwise. Social cohesion in small communities might be weakened by the disappearance of clear catchment areas defining a school's clientele, or by fierce competition between two neighbouring schools. Social polarisation may increase by the tendency of schools to be seen as "middle class" or "working class". Most seriously of all, in the case of support for private schools or of the creation of autonomous public schools, it is feared that choice will reduce the potential for improving public education as a system, and hence eventually harm its quality.

- *that choice in education is self-defeating*

Education, it is argued, differs from many commodities, in that one person's "consumption" may severely affect another's. Critics of choice point to the social nature of parents' aspirations: whom one goes to school with may be just as important as what happens when one gets there.[8] Moreover, where education is seen widely as a means of "getting ahead", and a good school is therefore a relative concept, it is by definition possible for only a proportion of choices to be met. Even where people's preferences are not mutually exclusive, there is scope for one choice affecting another – for example where a minority of parents choose not to send their children to a particular local school, which as a result becomes unviable and therefore unavailable to the majority who want it.

- *that putting power in the hands of consumers will create the "wrong" pressures for education*

Some critics of school choice fear that it might make education more conservative, by discouraging educators from introducing innovations that might not readily be understood by parents, who were educated a generation ago. They also claim that it will encourage schools to put their efforts into creating smart uniforms, clean buildings and glossy public relations, rather than good teaching.

Such fears derive to some extent from potential differences between the priorities and values of the majority of professional educators and of the majority of parents. But they are not based only on such differences. Parents have a tendency to use conventional criteria such as examination results when choosing the school that might determine their child's future chances, even if they support in principle the idea of educational innovation. A parent may not think that tidiness is the most important aspect of a school, yet still be strongly influenced by a school's appearance. In short, the sum of individual choices does not necessarily equal the collective will. This causes some to argue that parents' views can best be articulated through "voice" – for example by giving their elected representatives a say on school boards or governing bodies – rather than through "choice" at the individual level.

Characteristics of choice policies

Against this background of objectives and objections, public authorities have created a range of different policies that promote school choice. Not all of these policies have choice as their primary objective, and many have been introduced as part of broader programmes of educational reform with multiple aims. The country summaries in Part II of this report put policies in this context. However, it is useful here to define the main policies for school choice according to a broad classification:

Public support/toleration for non-public schooling

As already noted, no OECD country forbids the choice of private schools. However, the conditions under which governments are prepared to allow education to take place outside the public system varies considerably. In Sweden, for example, it is illegal for children to be schooled at home, or anywhere other than in a school that has been acknowledged by the National Agency for Education as providing a satisfactory curriculum. In the United States, over five million pupils attend private schools with minimal regulation, and home schooling is not only legal but has suddenly become a socially acceptable option: the Department of Education estimates that 350 000 children were schooled at home in 1992, compared to just 15 000 in the early 1980s.

Many countries, notably Denmark, the Netherlands and France, have a long history of providing public subsidies to schools in order to ensure choice. Support for the private option is sometimes seen implicitly or explicitly as justifying a public school system in which little or no school choice is permitted. But more recent policies to subsidise private education, proposed or adopted in countries such as Sweden, New Zealand and the United States, are intended to serve as a challenge to public schools by opening up competition. In these cases, they share a common objective with policies (described below) to increase competition within the public sector: to put pressure on public schools to take account of their customers' preferences.

Three key variables in public support for private schools are:

– *The method of support.* It is useful to distinguish support available mainly to certain kinds of school from support given on a formula basis to any school that applies for it. Support for religious schools in the Netherlands and France has been maintained under rules that require subsidised private schools to demonstrate that they have a distinctive character or philosophy not catered for in the public system; non-religious schools may apply, but they remain a small minority. At the other extreme, the rules adopted by Sweden's neo-liberal government in 1992 come close to a pure "voucher" system, under which money follows pupils directly to private schools regardless of their character. In Australia, subsidies are given independently of the character of the school; but by weighting subsidies according to a school means-test, and by means-testing Catholic schools as a group rather than individually, the system intentionally skews resources to this kind of school.
– *The level of support.* The effect of private school subsidy on choice depends crucially on whether it makes private schools affordable to most of the population. In the Netherlands it certainly does, as private schools are subsidised on the same level as public ones, and are forbidden to charge fees except for extra-curricular activities. At the other extreme, prestigious schools in Australia receive relatively small subsidies that make little impact on their fees of several thousand dollars a year. Sweden's per-pupil subsidy of 85 per cent of the cost of educating a child in the public system allows many schools to charge no fees. In Denmark, on the other hand, where the equivalent figure is 72 per cent, it is compulsory to

charge fees, on the basis that parents must show a commitment to a private school before it may be subsidised.
- *The permitted degree of independence.* Most private schools are allowed to pursue their own religious or educational principles regardless of subsidy, although in some countries such as France they are required to adhere to a strict national curriculum. Another aspect of control lies in finance: there is a big difference between on the one hand Sweden, Denmark and Australia, where money determined on a pupil-based formula is handed to schools to manage as they please, and on the other the Netherlands, where costs are financed directly by the State on the basis of equal educational provision for public and private schools. Indeed, it has been reasonably suggested that Dutch "private" schools are in reality no more private than religious schools in public systems such as Great Britain's (where they are "aided") and New Zealand's (where they are "integrated"). The most obviously private characteristics of Dutch schools – the private nature of their governance and their exemption from any local government planning process – increasingly apply to all schools in both Great Britain and New Zealand under policies that make them more independent.

Liberalised enrolment rules in the public sector

In most OECD countries, children have traditionally been allocated to public schools primarily according to where they live. Even in countries and parts of countries where there has not been a strict school zone, the notion of a "catchment area" from where a school draws its pupils has been strong, and in most cases remains so.

The basic element of any "open enrolment" policy is to give pupils the right, if it does not exist already, to enrol at any school. Such a right may be limited to schools within a local education authority, or may include transfer to another one, usually with provision for an equivalent transfer of public funds. But other important elements of enrolment rules include:
- *The terms in which the choice is presented.* There is a big psychological difference between Sweden, where pupils are still allocated a school but may choose a different one if they wish, and New Zealand, where nobody is steered towards any school. Only in the latter case are parents and pupils forced to think actively about which school to apply for.
- *The limits, if any, set on school rolls.* In the Netherlands there are none, and the public authorities need to build or procure extra accommodation for schools that are overcrowded. In New Zealand, schools are open to all until they actively demonstrate that they are in danger of overcrowding. In France, in places where choice of public secondary school is permitted, that choice is withdrawn not just if one's preferred school becomes too full, but also if one's local school becomes too empty.
- *The method of allocating school places when not all choices can be met.* The most common method, geographical proximity, can in some cases end up replicating the phenomenon that open enrolment is supposed to replace: the restriction of schooling by catchment area. However, the priority usually given to a child with a sibling at a school can weight provision in over-subscribed schools significantly towards out-of-zone families who enrolled at a time when there were still

spare places. New Zealand's enrolment schemes demonstrate how schools can potentially define their own client markets.[9] A radically different alternative used in a few school districts in the United States (see for example Case Studies 9 and 11) allocates places independently of residence. This is sometimes referred to as "universal choice". Allocation on a geographically neutral basis appeals to some Americans' idea of equal treatment, and is overlaid by the priority of balanced distribution of racial groups. But it can cause resentment among parents living close to a school who fail to get a place, and such methods seem unlikely to spread quickly within the United States or to other countries.

Policies encouraging schools to compete under liberal enrolment rules

No school likes to have empty classrooms, although some crowded ones may welcome a fall in pupil demand. For those who see school choice as the means of injecting the dynamic of competition into education, it is important to give schools the incentive to compete. The two complementary ways in which this is most commonly done is by linking school resources more closely to student numbers and by giving schools greater autonomy, especially in the financial sphere. These two measures need to be considered together, since the amount of resources controlled at the school level will influence how much is available to put into a pupil-based funding formula. The combination of financial autonomy and the possibility of enhancing resources by expanding rolls creates a dramatic change in the position of school leaders, whereby their destiny becomes controlled by parent and pupil choices rather than by administrative decisions.

In its simplest form, the "money follows pupils" principle involves a direct payment to each public school for each pupil enrolled. Four important characteristics of the way such arrangements work in practice are worth noting:

– First, the payment is always a proportion of the total funding of schools, with some money held back either to give to schools on a basis other than the number of pupils or to be spent directly by the governing authority. In England, where central government wants to concentrate as much money as possible on pupil-based funding, local authorities must delegate at least 90 per cent of school funding, of which at least 80 per cent must be pupil-determined. In Sweden, on the other hand, the municipality that pioneered pupil-based funding, Stockholm, links about 50 per cent of school budgets directly to enrolment.

– Second, the payment normally attaches the same value to each pupil enrolled. Choice policies have for this reason been accused of neglecting pupils with special needs. Yet some differential weighting is possible. In the Netherlands, for example, primary schools get extra teachers if they enrol a high proportion of children with poorly-educated parents – most of whom are immigrants.

– Third, the payment normally covers recurrent but not capital costs, which continue to be determined centrally. This is not surprising, given the different capital needs of schools with buildings of different age and in different state of repair. But as discussed elsewhere in this report, it limits the incentive to recruit extra pupils to the point where they fill existing buildings.

– Fourth, the payment relates to the average cost of educating a pupil, which is normally higher than the marginal cost. In other words, where an extra pupil can be admitted without the need to hire an extra teacher, the revenue that follows is a net gain for the school. This makes the incentive extremely powerful in such cases.

School choice does not necessarily, however, operate on the basis of delegated budgets based on pupil enrolments. The more managed Dutch system is an interesting alternative. Resources follow pupil demand, but are provided in kind rather than cash by the government: teachers and buildings, not guilders, are guaranteed to schools in proportion to their enrolments. It is interesting to note that while Dutch schools have less financial autonomy than many others, they have better prospects of seeing physical provision expanded to match demand.

In many countries, the trend towards school autonomy goes far beyond financial management. Self-governed public schools have been established universally in New Zealand, partially in the United Kingdom and experimentally in the United States. It is not in the scope of this report to consider governance as a separate subject. But it is important to note here the connection between devolution of responsibilities, the growing self-perception of schools as independent entities and their inclination to compete for pupils and to see themselves as players in a "market" rather than a managed system.

Policies enabling schools to be different under liberal enrolment rules

Opening up enrolment does not, in the first instance, increase variety among schools.[10] Inertia as well as real obstacles may prevent schools from developing particular educational characteristics. Certain central or local government initiatives have permitted, encouraged or decreed school specialisation:

- It is necessary to *permit* specialisation where curriculum or other rules would otherwise make it difficult. In Sweden's highly uniform school system, for example, the development of a particular "profile" by certain schools in the 1980s was preceded by a relaxation of specific national rules prescribing the number of lessons per week spent on each subject. It may be noted that in countries like Britain and the United States, where recent trends have been towards greater curriculum prescription, the scope for increased variety may be less than in a country like Sweden, where the trend is in the opposite direction.
- Governments may also *encourage* schools to exercise existing or newly-created powers to define a distinct identity. In its 1992 policy document on choice and diversity[11] the English government encouraged secondary schools to specialise where the curriculum permitted it, as well as announcing new rules to allow a business to sponsor technology specialisation in exchange for a role in governing a school. Encouragement tends to be most effective when accompanied by financial incentives, but this brings two risks: that the schools bidding for the money will not have a genuine commitment to the pedagogical change required, and that other schools will object to unequal treatment.
- But governments and education authorities also often *decree* diversity. This may sound rather surprising, except when set alongside the risk that simply permitting or encouraging it will not work. New Zealand announced in 1989 the possibility of converting a school into a "Designated Character School" at the initiative of 21 or more parents; by 1993 not a single application to do so had been received. In New South Wales, the establishment of specialised language and technology schools, which formed part of the state's policy of curriculum development in

these subjects, was implemented differently: the state government simply redesignated schools, to produce a well-distributed geographical network (see Case Study 6). Magnet school policies in the United States have also tended to be announced by local education authorities, although in most cases it is the school itself that must apply for magnet status. Like in New South Wales, diversity and choice have been used in the United States as an instrument to achieve another planned objective: in this case the racial desegregation of schools, through voluntary means rather than forced bussing. Finally, it is interesting to note that in the London borough of Wandsworth, a local authority plan to create a district-wide network of magnet schools was thwarted by the choice of most secondary schools to opt out of local government control. Thus the replacement of a co-ordinated school system with a fragmented school market may work against the creation of a greater range of choices.

Policies to make choosing schools more feasible

Having given parents the right to choose, given schools an incentive to compete and promoted a greater range of school choices, governments may also consider it necessary to facilitate the choice process itself. This may be particularly important if groups that have not traditionally exercised choice are to be encouraged to do so. In particular, governments may have a role in:

– *Providing independent information.* The British government has put a strong emphasis on publishing examination results and inspection reports in forms that are meaningful to parents. More directly, the establishment of parent information centres in Boston (see Case Study 11) is an example of how informal channels of information about schools can be supplemented by formal ones.
– *Assisting with transport.* Public assistance with school transport has tended, even after enrolment rules have been relaxed, to favour attendance of one's nearest school. New Zealand has devised a new system which provides greater neutrality without greatly increasing the public cost. Pupils at any school may receive a subsidy equal to the cost of transport to the nearest school, even if they travel further afield. In addition, schools may opt to receive transport subsidies for their pupils in bulk, allowing them to pay the full cost for more distant students if they need them to fill up their rolls.

Chapter 2 considers in more detail the case for such policies, in the context of the behaviour and constraints that determine how schools are chosen in practice.

Chapter 2
The Process of Choosing Schools: Patterns, Constraints and Policy Influences

Choosing a school can be a complex, emotive, arbitrary, high-stakes, difficult process. As parents increasingly get the message from the media, politicians and conventional wisdom that education determines a child's life-chances, the pressure to make the "best" available choice of school grows. Yet parents typically have little information about what will be best for their children. The criteria for decision-making are therefore frequently haphazard.

Does that matter? For those interested in school choice only as an aspect of individual freedom, the important thing is that parents' and pupils' preferences be respected, regardless of the basis for choosing. But for those who argue that school choice will help create more dynamic, purposeful schools, that it will give access to good education to those who have been denied it, or that it will create a new kind of educational pluralism, the ways in which choices are made will be vitally important. So before considering, in the next chapter, the degree to which choice achieves its purposes, it is necessary to look more closely at the choice process itself.

Parent's or child's choice?

School choice is frequently equated with parental choice. Indeed, most research studies of how choices are made consider only the parent's input into choosing a school. It is therefore difficult to assess reliably how much say is given to the person most directly affected: the pupil.

The importance of pupil preferences is an illustration of the limits to the market analogy in education. Pure market theorists tend to see the parent as consumer, the school as service-supplier and the pupil as occupying roughly the same market position as a car receiving a car-wash. Even leaving aside the question of children's rights, the attitude of a child can be essential to the effectiveness of his or her education. Moreover, in practice parents do seem to pay attention to their children's preferences, even if they do not give them the final say.

What evidence does exist indicates that choice of secondary schools in particular tends to be a joint decision between parents and pupils. In case-study research on the detailed impact of open enrolment in England,[12] an Open University research team found that 79 per cent of parents claimed that the first choice of secondary school was a joint decision between parent(s) and child. Only 2 per cent said the child had decided alone;

17 per cent that the parent(s) had decided alone. Research in London being carried out at King's College[13] confirms that pupils are usually involved in choice of secondary school, but suggests that middle-class parents are more likely than working-class ones to press their own choice onto their children where there is a conflict of preferences.

The role of children in choosing does of course vary according to age. Interviews of parents and pupils for the present study suggested that by the age of 11, pupils were at least equal choosers, and by the age of 14 they were starting to take a dominant role, in particular when choosing between schools meant deciding between programmes. Thus the degree of pupil involvement is partly determined by the structure of school systems. In countries like France and Sweden, where significant, subject-relevant choices of upper secondary school are required by all pupils at the age of 15 or 16, the pupil input tends to be greater than in countries where the last main choice of school is made at age 11 or 12. Thus two surveys carried out in 1988 and 1989 respectively found parents of 12 year-olds in Liège (Belgium) much less likely than parents of 15 year-olds in Paris (France) to make a unilateral choice of secondary school. In both countries the decision was usually a joint one, but the French children were more than four times as likely as their parents to make an independent decision (19.9 per cent and 4.4 per cent of all cases, respectively), whereas for the younger Belgians the parent decided more often (in 18 per cent of cases, rather than 13 per cent decided by the child).[14]

Although children entering primary school at age 5 to 7 are rarely presented with a direct choice among schools, their preferences can still be influential. As discussed in the following section, a school's atmosphere and the criterion of a child's happiness is a common feature of parental choice of school. In countries where schools are becoming more consumer-oriented as a result of competition, an increasing number of parents visit schools, often with their children, prior to making a choice.

Do children choose on different grounds from their parents? Parents and pupils interviewed in the Netherlands noted that physical aspects of the school – the "traditional" or "modern" aspect of the building, for example – tended to be important for children on school visits, while parents would base judgements more on conversations with the teacher. Where one's friends are going is clearly a key factor for many children moving from primary to secondary school. The King's College research cited above indicates that middle-class parents more actively transfer their own values regarding schooling to their children.

How many active choosers?

Even under policies to promote school choice, the pull of the nearest neighbourhood public school remains powerful. Transport considerations, the desire to go to school with neighbours and friends, the cost of private schooling and normal expectations mean that most children in most OECD countries attend the closest school unless there is a specific reason not to.

However, a number of factors have caused parents and pupils to choose otherwise. Dissatisfaction with specific public schools may be a growing consideration, although there is not firm evidence to show that this has increased generally. More probably, dissatisfaction with the local school or simply a preference for another is more likely than in the past to result in active choice, as schools are regarded rather as service-providers than as local institutions. The common public school, according to sociologist Robert Ballion, "seeks to express a universalism that no longer exists".[15] Greater mobility in terms of wider car ownership also helps reduce the physical constraint on choice.

So where policies open up the possibility of choice, either by allowing enrolment in non-assigned public schools or by making private schools cheaper or free to the user, a significant number of people appear to choose actively among schools. This number may represent a widely varying proportion of school pupils, depending on local cultures and conditions. In Sweden, according to one survey,[16] only 7 per cent of parents had ever chosen a school other than the neighbourhood one assigned to them; even in Stockholm, only 10 per cent made such a choice in the first year of open-enrolment rules. On the other hand in Boston (see Case Study 11), where enrolment procedures require every parent to make an active choice, fewer than half select a school classified as being within walking distance.

An important consideration to emerge from experience of school choice in practice is that *the proportion of "active choosers" does not have to be large to have a significant impact on school systems*. This is particularly true where schools' resources are directly linked to enrolment. If a public school loses 10 per cent of its pupil intake and therefore 10 per cent of its revenue, the impact is usually severe, as a class with 27 pupils does not cost less to teach than one with 30. The incentive for schools to compete for pupils under open enrolment rules is therefore usually great.

How are choices made, and by whom?

Research from different countries shows no single consistent picture in terms of how people make choices, nor of who are the most active choosers. One problem is the difficulty in prompting parents to define how they and their children make a choice which is generally complex. Another is that choices are so often particular to an individual situation – whether to the institutional arrangements of a country, the geographical considerations in a district, the special characteristics of a school or the personal characteristics of a child.

However, from often murky patterns it is possible to make a number of observations:

Many parents and pupils do not live close enough to more than one school to consider choice a reality

In Sweden, this applies to choice of private schools, which are heavily concentrated in urban areas, and to out-of-zone public schools, which are rarely chosen not just in the countryside but also in medium-sized towns. In Scotland, where choice patterns under conditions of open enrolment have been well researched, the number of requests for schools other than the local one varied in 1985 from over 16 per cent in Edinburgh to 1 per cent in some rural areas.[17] Only in a country like the Netherlands, which guarantees the right to establish separate schools for different religions and for secular education in every community where there is a specified minimum of demand, can choice become a reality in small towns and rural areas. As discussed in the Netherlands country summary in Part II, the heavy cost of such a system is encouraging the Dutch government to tighten the criteria for supporting small schools.

Choices are made by all social classes, but not always in the same way

The choice between public and private schools is often constrained by price, and therefore available mainly to the more affluent. But even where choice between schools does not involve a binding price constraint, it might potentially be exercised disproportionately by privileged classes, who have better access to information and transport and who have always been more effective at making the most of public services. In many countries where choices have been extended, the middle classes are perceived as having been the most active choosers. There is considerable evidence to show that this is so in particular situations, but no general evidence that the less privileged fail to make choices. Perhaps the differences between classes in terms of the manner of choosing are more revealing than differences in the amount of choosing. The following examples illustrate these points:

- Longitudinal research in Australia has suggested that the socio-economic advantages of upper-middle-class origins may repeat their effects in terms of secondary school choice for children.[18] Such evidence in the Australian context of subsidised private education applies in particular to the choice of independent schools, where there is an important price constraint, but far less to the mainly low-fee Catholic schools that account for over two-thirds of private school enrolments and are chosen by families from all social origins.
- The choice of the French *lycée* is clearly linked to the level of educational aspiration of families, which in turn is linked to social and professional status. Asked to rate their 15 year-old children's educational merits and potential, 85 per cent of managerial and professional parents said they were good or excellent, compared to 52 per cent of manual workers.[19] In a system where different high schools give different academic prospects, this has a direct effect on school choice. Another close link between choice and family background, common in many countries but particularly pronounced in France, is the more active choosing by parents who are teachers. Research on the effect of a policy to allow some French children to attend a lower secondary school outside their home catchment area found that 20 per cent who did so had at least one parent who was a teacher.[20]
- However, French upper middle-class families appear less likely to choose a lower secondary school outside their home catchment area than French lower middle-class-families.[21] The presumed explanation is that the latter are more likely to share neighbourhoods with working-class families, and the more desired schools are in "better" social areas. Choice is seen by aspiring parents as a route to upward mobility for their children.
- Scottish research shows, more clearly than any other, that school choice can be made across social classes. The most comprehensive study[22] could find no evidence to suggest that middle-class parents were making a disproportionate number of placement requests under open enrolment. But parents living on poor housing estates typically used choice to escape to schools in better neighbourhoods, whereas middle-class parents, not surprisingly, remained in familiar social settings. The authors argued that better-motivated working-class parents, who opted out of schools that they considered undesirable, helped to make them still less desirable. Since only 9 per cent of parents on average chose a school other than their local one, the great majority remained with this less-wanted option.

- In Milwaukee, Wisconsin, a limited number of poor children are given vouchers to attend private schools. Parents who use this to escape the public school system have more education than other poor parents and, crucially, include many of the "activists" who had pushed for change in public schools (see Case Study 15).
- In Montclair, New Jersey, where all parents can choose among "magnet" schools with different characteristics, people from all backgrounds make an active choice. But better-off parents tend to rely on more sources of information, and those who do so are on average more satisfied with the school that they select (See Case Study 9).
- Research being undertaken in London[23] suggests that separate "circuits" of schools with varying characteristics are considered by different parents. The researchers distinguish for example comprehensive schools with a local, community character from "cosmopolitan, high-profile, élite" schools which, although public, recruit some students from beyond their immediate locale and exercise varying degrees of selection. The key characteristic of these circuits is that parents who "belong" to one circuit tend not even to consider options in another, because they are not in the relevant information network that defines school reputations. Moreover, many working-class families' ignorance of the cosmopolitan circuit, though potentially limiting social mobility, cannot be considered purely as a handicap: "...many working-class parents want and value different things from their schools; localness is often a value in its own right. The priorities and possibilities of choice are significantly different for middle-class and working-class choosers".[24] It would be dangerous to assume that such a statement has a universal validity, but it is worth noting as an example of observed behaviour and expressed values.
- Preliminary results from another ongoing English study on choice of schools suggests that:

"...many working-class families are keen to have a range of both non-academic and academic opportunities, and possess a marked sensitivity towards how the school environment will affect their child and towards their child's own viewpoint of the environment. For professional and middle-class parents the overriding factor is an environment characterised by academic success and an atmosphere or ethos that supports this."[25]

In judging school quality, academic performance is only one of several important criteria

Those who claim that choice creates a new demand pressure for schools to "perform" well sometimes imply that schools are judged only according to their academic results. As illustrated in the quote immediately above, academic success can be rated differently by different groups. For all groups, crude measures of academic performance such as test scores seem to play a limited role. The atmosphere or ethos of the school seems to be at least as important, although whether this is valued for its effect on academic performance, on social behaviour or on a child's happiness is not always easy to distinguish. What might be called "situational" reasons – the location of the school, the attendance of a sibling or friends, and so on – also seem to play an important part in most cases. It should also be noted that "academic" factors seem to play a greater role in school choices for children as they get older. The Tables 1 to 4 are examples of how parent motives are ranked, in different countries and at different educational levels.

Table 1. **Reasons for choosing a Swedish compulsory school**
(Entry ages: 7, 10, 14)

Reason for choosing a school other than the nearest	Percentage of parents
Friends/good peer atmosphere	34
Quiet/not violent/small classes	21
Good teachers/school leadership	16
Social factors/attention to pupils	15
Special pedagogical character (Waldorf, Montessori, etc.)	12
Geographical factors	10
Better equipment/facilities	8
Attention to pupils with problems	7
Special subject character (music, art, foreign language)	5
Good reputation	5
Possibility of parent influence	4
Special religious character	2

Note: 7 per cent of a sample of Swedish parents said they had at some time chosen a school other than their nearest public one. These parents were asked to give reasons for their choice. The categories represent summaries of reasons given spontaneously.
Source: Temo Testhuset Marknad Opinion, *op. cit.*, note 16.

Table 2. **Reasons for choosing an English secondary school (%)**
(Entry age: 11)

	An influential reason	One of the three most important reasons
Child preferred school	59.2	23.3
Near to home/convenient for travel	57.3	23.7
Children's friends will be there	56.1	14.5
Standard of academic education	55.7	21.0
Facilities	55.7	20.6
School's reputation	54.6	20.6
Child will be happy there	49.2	21.0
School atmosphere	44.7	5.0
Policy on discipline	42.0	11.5
Standard of education in non-academic areas	40.8	6.5
Examination results	38.9	11.1
What school teaches/subject choices	37.4	6.9

Note: 18 other reasons, of lesser importance, were given. Parents were selecting from a number of secondary schools in an English town.
Source: P.A. Woods (1993), *op. cit.* note 12.

Table 3. **Reasons for choosing a French lycée (%)**
(Entry age: 15)

	Most important reason	One of three most important reasons
Success at *baccalauréat*	6.2	10.4
Quality of teaching	15.0	20.3
Reputation	13.7	25.1
Discipline	0.7	3.3
Total of above 4 motives[1]	35.6	59.1
Smaller classes	2.0	4.3
Subject option	14.7	20.9
Atmosphere	1.0	6.9
Continuity	10.7	16.2
Closeness	27.0	51.7
Sibling(s)	2.6	10.1
Child's preference	6.5	12.4
Total	100.0	181.6

1. The author comments that the first four motives, which might be considered as representing judgements of a school's "value", were cited at least once by 59.1 per cent of respondents, but represent only one-third of all reasons given.
Note: 38.4 per cent of respondents gave no second reason, and 84.1 per cent gave no third reason. The parents had children who had recently entered a *lycée* after attending a *collège* (lower-secondary school) in Paris's 12th *arrondissement*.
Source: R. Ballion (1989), *op. cit.* note 14.

Table 4. **Factors considered as important in choosing a school, by United States parents**

Very or fairly important factors	Percentage agree
Quality of teaching staff	96
Maintainance of school discipline	96
Curriculum/courses offered	95
Size of classes	88
Grades/test scores of students	88
Close proximity to home	74
Extracurricular activity	68
Athletic programme	53
Racial or ethnic composition	32

Source: "Survey of the public's attitude towards the public school". *Phi Delta Kappan*, September 1991.

Religious characteristics of a school are of diminishing importance in many countries, but are sometimes a proxy for other characteristics

The association of public education with secular education once made religion the central issue of school choice in many countries. The choice of schools with a religious identity survived under varying conditions – unsubsidised (in the United States), subsidised (in the Netherlands, Belgium, France, and Australia since the 1970s) or integrated into the public sector (in Germany, the United Kingdom, and New Zealand since the

1970s). The growing secularisation of society, together with rising educational costs, has threatened the survival of religious schools that lack public support: in the United States the number of Catholic school enrolments has fallen from 5.5 million in 1962 to 2.6 million in 1992 (although this drop has been partly offset by growth in evangelical and Jewish schools). Yet where religious schools are available at little or no cost to families, they continue to enjoy popularity.

The most striking example of this is in the Netherlands. Between 1947 and 1988, the proportion of the population who did not belong to any church doubled from 17 per cent to 32 per cent. But private (though publicly funded) religious schools continued to be chosen by the majority of the population: between 1950 and 1990, Christian primary schools declined from 71 per cent to 63 per cent of enrolments, but Christian secondary schools rose from 38 per cent to 64 per cent. It is clear that many people choose confessional schools in the Netherlands and elsewhere for reasons other than religion – many "religious" schools have only a minority of adherents from their own faith. The most frequent reason seems to be choice of their ethos, which is sometimes perceived to be more in keeping with a family's values than the secular system.

Catholic schools are in many countries, including France, Australia and the Netherlands, perceived to offer a familial atmosphere in which the character and development of the individual is given attention. In a country like France, where public schools put much stress on academic discipline and achievement, this difference is welcomed by parents whose children fail to fit in. In countries like the United Kingdom and the United States, where discipline in the public system is a major issue, the roles are to some extent reversed: some parents opt for religious schools in search of greater order. Thus schools with a religious identity are offering an alternative that may be chosen not just by the religiously-motivated, but by people who dislike the style of secular education, rather than the secularism itself. As the scope of school choice expands, religious schools are likely to be a popular vehicle for the formulation of non-religious choices.

It must, however, be noted that while the established religions have dwindling congregations in most OECD countries, new ones are emerging. In particular, Islamic migrants and converts to "new Christian" faiths are growing rapidly in number. They have found it hard to establish schools in an already established school system. Many new Christian schools have started up in the United States, Australia and Sweden, but they are usually very small and often of fragile viability. A central problem for these schools, especially in countries with a strong national curriculum, is cultural clash with the main education system and, indeed, with the largely secular cultures to which devout followers of those religions object. It is these schools that will test how far new forms of school choice will permit variations in schooling based on religious differences. An early test may come in Sweden, where the principle of freely available vouchers for private schools is to be subjected to inspection to ensure that they are delivering a satisfactory education.

Where the "common" school's status diminishes, "uncommon" characteristics sometimes become attractive

The neighbourhood school, attended by all children in an area, risks in some cases suffering the same fate as the local grocer's shop. Most people like the idea of its closeness and friendliness, but as increasing numbers are tempted by benefits of shopping elsewhere, its quality declines and the trickle away from it becomes a flood. In most schools in most countries, enough people see the advantages of choosing locally, or lack realistic alternatives, for the outflow to remain at most a trickle. However, as discussed above, a substantial and growing proportion look actively at the qualities offered by a range of schools. Having broken with the idea of attending a school because it is the "normal" option, these choosers are inclined to look for something that is special.

In a small minority of cases, mainly at the primary level, they choose schools offering a coherent alternative pedagogy, such as Montessori or Waldorf/Steiner schools. The difficulty of running such schools within a public framework may account for their relative rareness; in the Netherlands, where they can be provided free by the private, subsidised sector, they are growing rapidly. However, most parents are reluctant to subject their children to anything that seems "experimental", and at the secondary level in particular are influenced by conventional definitions of educational success.

A different way to be special is for a school to declare a particular emphasis in its programmes. This approach has become especially common in the United States, where "magnet" schools offer special features such as a maths and science emphasis, a performing arts programme or a programme for the "gifted and talented". "Profile schools" in Sweden, "city technology colleges" in England and specialised schools in New South Wales are other examples of this phenomenon, described in case studies (Part III).

What is interesting about this type of development is that schools identifying a special characteristic seem to become more popular almost regardless of the extensiveness or quality of their difference. In some cases, the announcement of a defining characteristic is little more than a marketing tool, identifying an existing strength. In others, the changes are real, but it is the special*ness* as much as the special*ism* that seems to influence parents. Research on choice of England's city technology colleges indicates that reasons for choosing them are "no more often a straightforward choice of a distinctively technological form of secondary education than a reflection of more general factors", such as perceived high academic standards associated with a much-publicised, well-resourced school.[26]

A significant influence in choosing a school is who else chooses it

Nobody likes choosing a school that is considered by one's friends to be undesirable. Few privileged families wish their children to attend schools mainly with children from less privileged backgrounds. Many parents believe, despite mixed academic evidence on this point, that their child will learn better alongside other children who are clever than in a mixed-ability setting.

Such considerations, and particularly those associated with race and class, do not tend to show up directly in surveys of reasons for choosing schools. Few people like to admit to social or racial prejudice. However, they are prominent in the assessments of why parents choose made by many head teachers and local officials interviewed for this study. Moreover, more probing studies of how parents choose[27] reveal a strong social element to choice. Sometimes this component is mixed up with or implied in other expressed motives, such as liking the school's atmosphere, or children's desire to be with their friends.

The rush to enrol in some schools that acquire "special" characteristics may be explained partly by the idea that they will attract a "good" intake, whether socially or academically. In some cases, where the intake is consciously balanced by race (as in magnet schools), social background or ability (as in city technology colleges), such images may not be justified. But a desire to cluster in what are agreed to be the "best" schools is also attributable to the phenomenon, observable outside theatres, of a queue to get in being a sign of quality. The statement attributed to Groucho Marx, of having no wish to belong to a club with standards low enough to accept him as a member, has some pertinence to school choice. In a school district where enrolment is open but places in popular schools rationed by residence, a parent may have no wish to send a child to a non-local school empty enough to accept that child, as the spare place would illustrate that it was not popular.

Policy responses: choice, geography and transport

Geography can limit or pre-empt school choice in a number of ways.

In a system in which children are allocated to schools on a strictly residential basis, the only way to choose a school in the public system is to move house. In geographically mobile societies, notably the United States, selecting schools by choosing residence is a common activity, with the wealthiest families being able to bid for housing near the best schools. In the American context in which schools are financed, unequally, by often tiny school districts, moving to a wealthy district means schools that are not only free of social problems but also benefit from a high tax base.

In a system that allows pupils to enrol in any public school, the principle of greater choice will in reality be limited by a number of geographical factors. As noted at the end of the previous section, where popular schools continue to select students on the basis of geography, access to a desired distant school may be prevented. Where places are available, the question of travel to the school arises. In many rural areas, families typically consider only one school as accessible to their homes. In urban areas where a greater range of options are available, the following travel-related considerations may be relevant:

- Does a more distant school involve extra expense? In some countries (*e.g.* England, New Zealand) the cost of transport has been covered only to the nearest appropriate school.
- Does a more distant school require extra parental travel time? A large proportion of families have either two working parents or a lone parent. Most parents seek a school close enough to walk to or accessible by a bus near to the child's home.
- Is the method of getting to school safe? For children who walk alone, violence, abduction and traffic threats have become major worries in many cities.

These factors can cause varying patterns in different situations. In the United States, an extensive school bus system improves options considerably, especially where walking to school is considered dangerous. This can cause a perverse situation where a *more* distant school requires less parental time, as a minimum distance is required before a bus is provided (see Case Study 11). In the Netherlands, the bicycle provides a flexible and (in the context of bicycle-oriented traffic management) safe means of getting to school, and significantly enhances the degree of secondary school choice.

Public policy may potentially be used to reduce, although it will never eliminate, the constraints of geography on school choice. It is evident that permitting enrolment in a school outside one's local zone on its own can go only a small way towards extending geographical choice. Other means of doing so may include:

- *Priorities for admitting children to over-subscribed schools other than local residence.* As noted in Chapter 1, policies removing all links between local residence and admission may be socially and politically unacceptable. However, as American magnet schools have illustrated, it is quite possible for a school to allocate some places to local children and others on a system-wide basis, on social, racial or other criteria. Where school choice policies aim to broaden educational opportunities, such measures need to be considered.
- *Changing rules on transport assistance as part of a policy for school choice.* New Zealand's change in subsidy rules, described at the end of Chapter 1, came five years after school zones were abolished. Where children rely heavily on school buses, as in the United States, the structure of such provision may need to be reassessed with the extension of school choice. The system that might most efficiently give the greatest choice is for buses to take all children in a district from near their homes to a central location, and from there to each of the district's schools. But the advantages in terms of choice of such a system need to be weighed against the greater amount of time that children will on average spend travelling, and the social desirability of daily passing thousands of children through a giant mustering station.
- *Purposely siting more desirable schools in less privileged districts.* This has been done in the case of some American magnet schools and of England's city technology colleges. Such policies have gone some way towards providing opportunities for children excluded from some other schools for geographical reasons, but their controlled admissions policies can sometimes seem to limit choices for local residents. A magnet school in a black area may, because of the aim of racial balance, only have spare places available for Whites. City technology colleges recruit pupils from a wide area on the basis of their motivation and other criteria (see Case Study 7), and thus can be inaccessible to some families living nearby.
- *Guaranteeing choice of school for local communities.* The Netherlands does this systematically by allowing a fully-funded private school of a particular religion or philosophy to start up in any community that does not have one, where demand can be demonstrated. Sweden and Denmark also have rules allowing high subsidies to private schools that may be considered too small to be viable in the public system. The Dutch policy makes the choice of more than one school a reality in many small communities; the Danish and Swedish policies sometimes sustain the choice of a local school in a village that may otherwise not have one. Such policies may add to the total cost of schooling, but may be seen as meeting an important social need.

Policy responses: choice and information

The fact that parents who are teachers make more active use of school choice highlights the constraint on other choosers posed by lack of information. There are two reasons why governments might want to see an improvement in the flow of information to parents and pupils. First, because uneven access to information for choosing schools tends to favour families that are already privileged educationally. Second, because in the absence of solid information on school performance, choices will be made on an arbitrary basis that fails to create demand-side incentives for schools to make genuine educational improvements.

Information can be made available in a variety of ways. A first step in many countries is to encourage schools to become more open to parents and to prospective ones. Schools in different countries come from very different starting points. In most English-speaking countries there is a degree of openness to outsiders, especially in primary schools, which has been strengthened by the increasing use of adults as helpers in classrooms. In a number of Continental European countries, parents have been kept at more of a distance and find it difficult to make direct judgements of schools. In Sweden, where school choice has been motivated to a considerable extent by the complaint that parents were never listened to, schools provided little information until the early 1990s, when they were required to produce an annual report for parents. In Sweden and in other countries where competition between schools has increased, this in itself has provided a strong incentive to provide information to prospective parents. After the choice-oriented reforms in the late 1980s in New Zealand and England, the number of open evenings and school brochures multiplied.

But as schools become more market-oriented, they also become better at presenting themselves in a favourable light. Parents may benefit from more neutral information. Most local education authorities supply little more than the name and a brief description of each school in the area. Parent information centres in Boston (described in Case Study 11) try to go much further. An obvious limitation of such centres is that they cannot give subjective judgements on the quality of individual schools. But they can help to ensure that a parent's search for a school is conducted on the basis of accurate information and a broad understanding of what is available.

A further means of giving parents information is to publish indicators of school performance or inspection reports. In England, the government has made the publication of such information a central principle of education policy. One element of this policy is the publication of school examination results, amid heated controversy. Another is a reform of the inspection system to produce reports that aim to be helpful to parents in making choices.

A combination of the information sources identified in this section can improve the basis on which choices of schools are made. The debate over publication of "league tables" of English schools' exam results centred on the desirability of ranking schools according to a single indicator, which took no account of factors such as the abilities of a school's pupil intake. The more information is available, the less likely is one factor to have an undue or arbitrary influence on a school's popularity.

Chapter 3

The Impact of Choice

What effect does school choice have on education? This broad question will never be answered satisfactorily, because choice is but one of many influences on educational development, whose effects are hard to distinguish from others'. What seems clear, however, is that some forms of choice have important consequences for the environment in which schools operate, and hence for the educational process. This chapter considers a number of aspects of schooling on which choice might have an impact.

Choice and educational quality

It is unlikely that research will ever prove or disprove a relationship between school choice or competition on the one hand, and improvement in the quality or effectiveness[28] of schools on the other. The world is not a laboratory; differences between systems that do and do not allow choice are accompanied by so many other differences that the impact of choice is impossible to disentangle. Yet the doctrine that schools will be better if they are more competitive is so central to the policy debate in a number of countries that the case for believing in such a link has to be examined.

The firmest and most frequently-cited evidence claimed to support the case for choice relates to differences in effectiveness between school sectors. In the United States, a deep controversy was provoked in 1982 when James Coleman and others produced evidence appearing to show that American private high schools were more effective than public ones.[29] Evidence from the Netherlands shows that in certain cases denominational schools are more effective than others.[30] In the United Kingdom, the new "grant-maintained" sector (public, but divorced from local government control) is being closely watched, although preliminary evidence found improvements in this sector broadly in line with trends elsewhere.[31]

Even where differences between sectors can be demonstrated, they do not necessarily prove that greater freedom to choose the successful sector would improve schooling overall. First, the effect of such choice on the schools that remain in the less successful sector is uncertain. Secondly, it is difficult for any research to control fully for varying characteristics of students in different sectors. Thirdly, a sector may have other distinctive characteristics which are not easy to duplicate. Coleman and Hoffer found in 1987[32] that higher effectiveness of Catholic schools could be attributed to stronger ties between parents and schools and the role of the Church as an intergenerational community around the school. In the Netherlands, where denominational schools are now attended by a wide range of pupils no longer held together by religious communities, nor distinguished by higher income or ability, such differences are less obvious. Research suggests, however, that denominational schools are more effective in areas of the Netherlands such as Groningen and Amsterdam where they are chosen as the exception, rather than in areas such as the South where they are the norm.[33] A school that is abnormal may have advantages, such as a stronger than average sense of identity, and more powerful links with its clients, who have made more of a conscious decision about schooling than those who conform to the norm. Coherence of mission also shows up as an important contributor to Catholic school effectiveness in the United States.

Whilst such evidence on different sectors does not prove that more choice will improve education, it points to certain features of schools associated with effectiveness which might also be associated with school choice. The dynamic created by parents' and pupils' choosing and by schools having to compete for enrolments might potentially contribute to effectiveness by:
- strengthening school leadership and sense of mission;
- improving parental identification with the school chosen, and parental involvement with the school;
- improving pupil motivation, where pupils have made a conscious choice.

All of these characteristics are evident in certain individual schools operating under new policies for choice. In particular, under new conditions of competition within the public sector in England, New Zealand and Sweden, schools became much keener to define their mission, and head teachers often acquired a stronger role – also associated with the parallel policy of devolution of responsibilities to schools. The degree to which such responsibilities create more effective leadership can depend on how well head teachers and others are prepared for these new roles.

But competition might also have a negative influence on the educational effectiveness of schools. In the perception of many teachers in those countries where it has increased, competition has been a diversion from education, since the most effective way to compete for pupils at the margin is through relatively superficial (even though desirable) measures such as the effective presentation of the school to parents, or the creation of a clean, orderly environment.

A further possibility is that the kind of school leadership encouraged by school choice, and by the devolution of administrative and financial responsibility to schools, will not necessarily improve educational effectiveness. Growing management responsibility has been associated with a diminishing involvement of some head teachers in their school's educational mission. The degree to which such leadership can be effectively delegated is an open question. Future research on school effectiveness may do well to distinguish more precisely the contribution of different types of school leadership, and of the relationships between a school's management and teaching staff.

Choice and the relationship between schools and parents

Neo-liberal ideology sees school choice as a redefinition of relationships between schools as "producers" of education and parents as "consumers". Once parents have the power of exit, educators have to pay more attention to their preferences, rather than running schools simply according to professional judgements of what is good for pupils. In a country like Sweden, where parents have felt that their wishes have been systematically ignored by schools, the introduction of a right to choose another school appears to have started to redress this balance.[34]

However, there is a vital difference between parent-school relationships and the consumer-producer relationship in most commercial transactions. Consider the following three types of parental influence:

- *consumer pressure*: schools competing for enrolments adjust their behaviour in ways that they believe will appeal to parents as customers;
- *parent involvement*: parents participate directly in the day-to-day operation of schools, which listen to their suggestions and encourage them to become partners in the education of their children;
- *parent governance*: parents or their representatives are given a contributing or a decisive say in the governance of schools.

In the first of these types, parents act merely as consumers. In the other two, they are also co-producers. Parent governance has been a significant recent development in British and New Zealand schools, and a long-standing feature of Danish "free" schools. In Denmark, the stipulation that these subsidised private schools must be controlled by parents is closely linked to the principle of choice, in ensuring that subsidies only go to institutions with a genuine parental commitment (see Case Study 14). However, in general the question of governance is distinct from that of school choice: in principle, it entails the power of "voice" as distinct from the power of choice or "exit".[35]

With parent involvement, however, the roles of parents as "consumers" and as "producers" potentially become complementary. This is possibly the most powerful as well as constructive form of parent influence, as it combines the parent's importance as a client of the school with a growing contact with and understanding of the educational process itself. School principals in Stockholm say they are putting increasing stress on involvement with parents, knowing that they will be the best advertisers to attract more enrolments in the school. The duplication in public, secular schools of the "intergenerational community" observed in private religious ones can potentially combine an increase in parental satisfaction with an increase in school effectiveness.

Choice and educational values

Parental influence has sometimes been seen, particularly by Conservatives, as a counterbalance to the values of professional educators in determining the character of education. In particular, according to this premise, certain new ideas introduced into education in recent years have deviated from a traditional model of sound education and left parents confused and unsatisfied. One reason for believing that parents will exert a conservative influence is that their knowledge of education stems from their own school days, a generation previously.

In practice, the direction of parental influence seems to depend heavily on the way it is exercised. Parental involvement tends to create a closer understanding between parents and teachers, which reduces the chance of a clash in values. Consumer pressure alone, on the other hand, appears to have the potential to influence schools in a generally conservative direction. One reason for this has been discussed in the section on "Objections" in Chapter 1. Even progressively-minded parents are sometimes inclined to apply conventional criteria to choice of their own children's school, because they believe that their children's success in life will be determined by society's conventional values. Parents are also inclined to place attention on fundamental values high on the list of desired school attributes, and to regard with suspicion changes that seek to question or challenge central tenets of society. Some commentators believe that it is schools' duty to reflect such wishes of parents. Others believe that schools should have a more questioning role with respect to society's values. It is also possible that conservative pressures might make schools dull and unadventurous in their pedagogy, even if they are bold in their marketing. It is interesting to note that one of the biggest changes in English schools, to a casual observer, in the years following the liberalising of enrolment policies was the large-scale adoption of dress codes and uniforms.

Public subsidies for significant private school sectors in France, the Netherlands, Sweden and Australia amongst other countries help create a degree of pluralism in values. As discussed in Chapter 2, this can go beyond religious beliefs even in the case of religiously-defined schools, by allowing parents to opt for schools with a distinctive moral or social atmosphere. Yet systems of choice have not on the whole encouraged a large diversity in educational approach, other than in a relatively small number of schools espousing alternative pedagogical philosophies, such as Montessori schools. Denmark is a notable exception: its "free" schools permit every kind of ideology from highly conservative to highly liberal, and encourage experimentation with educational ideas.

In the Netherlands, outside a small if growing number of secular private schools (mainly primary) associated with alternative pedagogies, the power to choose has if anything militated against educational experimentation. In his background report to this study,[36] Dronkers suggests that religious schools appeal to parents partly because of their "mild educational conservatism" on average, because parents do not like experimentation with their own children. Some Dutch religious school spokesmen dispute that they are more conservative (as Dronkers points out, "conservative" is not a popular term in the Netherlands). However, it is clear that choice has on occasions hindered efforts for change in the Dutch school system – especially efforts in recent years to make the secondary school system more "comprehensive". The Case Study 1 on Haarlem in Part III illustrates how school behaviour has been affected by many parents' preference for schools where their children mix as little as possible with children of lower abilities. At the macro level, system-wide change in secondary education is difficult to achieve when over 70 per cent of schools are controlled privately.

Choice and programme diversity

In the East Harlem district of New York City, students entering junior high school can choose freely among schools with a wide range of educational programmes, from a heavy emphasis on mathematics and science to specialism in the performing arts, and from open classrooms with high parental participation to traditional teaching settings. Most of these programmes are delivered by small schools, sometimes occupying only part of a school building, and delivered by innovative teachers who have been allowed to put their educational ideas into practice. The result is to offer parents and pupils, in a district that might otherwise contain only "sink" schools, an exceptional range of real educational choices.[37]

Although East Harlem's experience is the result of innovation started in the 1970s, and the subject of many research studies and newspaper articles published around the world, there have been a notable lack of attempts to copy it. One reason is that the initiative was started neither as part of an administratively-imposed programme nor in response to demand from parents, but at the initiative of local educational visionaries, whose aim was to put their own ideas into practice. It is therefore not easily transplanted.

Giving parents free choice of school does not on its own seem to encourage genuine programme diversity. As noted in Chapter 2, schools which advertise their programme strengths by adopting a label, such as "music school", seem to enhance their popularity. But particularly in countries that put a large stress on a common curriculum, schools tend to be reluctant to advertise themselves to a "niche" market, as they fear that specialising too much in one area might frighten other "customers" away.[38] One reason is because of the rareness of a structural feature of East Harlem: the operation of "mini-schools", more than one to a building, in a densely-populated area. This allows schools to offer programmes that appeal to only a fraction of people who have access to the school. A large comprehensive school competing with at the most one or two others for local residents cannot afford such a luxury.

An alternative has been for programme diversity to be created from the supply side, not as in East Harlem by opening up schools to local innovators, but by introducing system-wide networks of special-feature schools. Policies to do this have not always been motivated mainly by the desire to enhance choice for its own sake. American magnet schools were usually created by district authorities, initially to achieve a more even racial balance through voluntary enrolment decisions rather than compulsory allocation. Specialised schools in New South Wales (Case Study 6) are closely linked with centrally-directed curriculum reform. City technology colleges in England (Case Study 7) aim to enhance choice for children living in the inner city, but also to promote the status of technology in secondary schooling.

An obvious limitation on schools with particular subject programmes is the widespread view that most children should follow a balanced curriculum. In many European countries, government specification of which subjects should be studied underpins this uniformity. The United States, where the fashion of the "shopping mall high school" is being replaced (at least in rhetoric) by that of the common curriculum, and the United Kingdom, which introduced a national curriculum for the first time in 1988, are moving in this direction. But this does not prevent schools from creating programmes that innovate in particular subjects, or have an approach to subjects like technology that affects the whole curriculum.

Potentially, where such school-based innovation is combined with the right of parents and pupils to select it, choice can become a significant element of educational development. Innovation has a better chance of working on willing volunteers than on designated guinea-pigs.

Choice and the stakes for schools

In the late 1980s, three countries in this study adopted significant reforms motivated by the political idea that schools should be subject to the discipline of the marketplace. But in neither New Zealand, Sweden nor the United Kingdom has the full logic of that idea been carried through. Popular schools have gained resources, and unpopular schools have lost them as a result of enrolment trends. But unlike in a true market, the structure of supply has remained broadly constant.

The reason is straightforward. Governments need to ensure that every child has somewhere to go to school, and regulate accordingly the opening and closing of schools, as well as any significant expansion in physical capacity. In a situation where overall school rolls are not expanding, it is not financially efficient to increase places at a popular school and to close a less popular one. In most cases it is not politically popular either, as even less desired schools usually retain a majority of their pupils, if only for geographical reasons.

As a result, the "money follows pupils" idea has most frequently been applied to schools' recurrent income rather than capital. This has allowed schools in the public sector to attract extra resources only by increasing enrolments within physical capacity. That does not make the stakes for schools negligible: the opportunities afforded by enhancing income at the margin, and the risk of pupil losses necessitating reductions in teaching staff, have produced powerful incentives to schools to compete for pupils. But once a school is full, extra popularity tends to result mainly in the frustration of some choices caused by the need to accept pupils on a selective basis.

The corollary of popular schools' inability to expand is a limit to how far less popular schools are likely to contract. Empty places at schools will exist only to the extent that there is over-capacity in the system. In some such cases (see for example Maidstone in Case Study 3), open enrolment will produce an important indicator when decisions to close schools are taken; in cases where rolls are rising, in contrast (see Bradford, Case Study 2), most schools will be filled up regardless of their popularity.

This raises three significant questions for the design and operation of "choice" policies:

- *How do authorities respond to less popular schools?* If the norm is for such schools to stay open, possibly accepting pupils who have not succeeded in getting into other schools, there is a case for giving them extra attention to help them improve. In Montclair, New Jersey (Case Study 9), the school district intervenes to consider a change in character of schools whose rolls are falling. In New Zealand, Educational Development Initiatives (Case Study 16) look for new ways of structuring provision to help all schools to improve. In Stockholm (Case Study 4), the municipal authorities help failing schools to improve their programmes. Such efforts usually stop short of providing a perverse incentive: linking development money directly to low enrolment. But intervention to help less desired schools to improve may become an important part of any choice policy.
- *Is there a case for linking school expansion to popularity?* Expansion was not an issue in most countries in the 1980s, as school rolls were generally falling. But in the late 1990s and early 2000s the school-age population will rise in many OECD countries,[39] presenting a need for greater school provision in some areas. Linking capital resources directly to school enrolments is likely to cause inequities among

schools that start off with buildings of different ages and in different condition. But that does not mean that school provision needs to be planned on purely administrative or political criteria. A logical corollary of allowing parents to choose schools would be a clear commitment to give priority when expanding school provision to increase places at schools that were over-subscribed. However, the desire of successful schools to expand may be a significant constraint – especially where the character of a school is closely linked to its size. It may simply not be possible to meet the wishes of all parents who would like their children to attend a particular school because it is small and friendly.
 – *What kind of pupil selection will result from "school choice" policies?* This is the subject of the following section.

The above discussion about whether capital as well as recurrent income should follow demand applies in principle not just to public schools but to private ones. In Sweden, pupil-based subsidies to private schools relate to current rather than capital costs. But private schools often have greater flexibility in raising their own money for capital, as well as being eligible for various capital grants. Australia's New Schools Policy (see country summary in Part II) funds the start-up of new private schools where there is genuine new demand in a town or district; in the Netherlands, similar conditions apply, in both the public and the private sector. In Denmark, capital funds for private schools are now provided on a per-pupil basis. It would seem illogical if, in any country, subsidies for recurrent funding were to follow pupils to both sectors, but unequal access to capital enabled only private schools to expand to meet demand.

Choice and selection

The freedom of parents to choose schools is often restricted by the necessity for schools to choose pupils. For any school that is chosen by more pupils than it is willing or allowed to accept, some method must be used to decide who shall attend. Under zoned enrolment policies, schools are generally open to anybody living in the catchment area; a rise in pupil numbers results either in new building or overcrowding. The Netherlands is one of the few non-zoned countries that keep public school rolls open to all comers; in cases where one school in a municipality is overcrowded but the system has spare places, this can lead to classrooms in one school being used to teach children from another (see Case Study 1).

As discussed under "Choice, geography and transport" in Chapter 2, the most common method of restricting places in full schools is by location. But having broken the systematic link between schools and neighbourhoods, open enrolment policies raise the question of whether schools might select according to other criteria. Should pupils be concentrated in schools by ability or special aptitude for certain subjects? Should pupils be systematically distributed within districts to ensure a better social or racial balance than would have been achieved on a neighbourhood basis? Or should competing preferences be adjudicated on an entirely random basis? Such questions are answered in different countries according to local values and objectives.

A central consideration is who decides on the criteria for admission. In the United States, admissions criteria and procedures tend to be determined by the district authorities even when zoning is abolished, although in East Harlem, referred to above, schools have a say in admissions. (But the most common policy issue in school attendance, race, has been adjudicated by the American courts, which have served a large number of district-wide desegregation orders in recent years.) In England, local authorities have also controlled admissions criteria; schools that "opt out" of their control can determine their own admission arrangements subject to the Secretary of State's agreement. But the process of admission in that case passes more squarely to the school. Research into the first 100 grant-maintained schools[40] found that 30 per cent of those designated "comprehensive" were subjectively using school reports, parental or pupil interviews or examinations to help select pupils.

New Zealand stands out as a country that has given admissions criteria explicitly to individual schools. A school threatened with overcrowding can apply for permission to set up an enrolment scheme that gives it freedom to admit whom it chooses, as long as it publishes its policy and does not contravene human rights laws. As explained in the New Zealand summary in Part II, it is possible under such conditions to allow almost unlimited discretion over the admission of any individual, by listing a number of criteria that will be taken into account, but not specifying any order of priority. Under such circumstances, a popular public school becomes free to define its clientele – and, by exclusion, those of less popular neighbouring schools too. This changes the essential nature of public schools as part of a network that systematically provides educational opportunities for all children. It makes public schools much more like private ones.

One of the central objections to subsidies to private schools in many countries is that they are allowed to select their pupils. The degree to which they do so varies considerably, and many religious schools have adopted an inclusive attitude, not least out of a need to keep up numbers in order to remain viable. But the more prevalent that private schools become in a country, the greater the chance that there will be a concentration of problematic children in public ones, which will become less desirable as a result. In the development of school autonomy in a country like New Zealand, the possiblity that the same division will emerge between selective and open schools within the public sector – creating uneven distribution of educational opportunities – needs to be considered.

Choice and educational opportunities

As noted in Chapter 1, school choice policies sometimes aim to extend educational opportunities, particularly to those for whom choices have been limited. For those who have this objective, it is not enough to create an educational market. The results of that market for equity in education are also of interest.

The possibility that more privileged parents will be more active choosers has been discussed in Chapter 2. Although it is not inevitable that the benefits of school choice will accrue mainly to those whose educational opportunities are already high, there is a real danger that this will happen. This can be true even where all social classes are equally active in choice, because of a conjunction of three factors:[41]

- Schools in more affluent areas are usually considered more desirable than those in poorer areas.
- Only a minority of children usually end up outside their area of residence.
- Schools that are more popular in a choice system get more resources and therefore tend to improve, while less chosen ones deteriorate.

The result is that while some poorer pupils may escape their environment, most are left in schools at risk of losing resources because of choice, while pupils from richer families remain in the schools that benefit.

Ways in which the association between geography and educational opportunity might be reduced have been reviewed above, in the penultimate section of Chapter 2. Another approach is to see private schools as a good-quality alternative for poor children which does not require them to move around.

Concern to assure the link between choice and equity has been strongest in the United States, where one element of the choice movement originates from the political "left", and has intellectual roots in the civil rights movement of the 1960s. One way that some members of this group propose to expand choices for the disadvantaged is by helping more of them to go to private schools, and in particular to the small, often religious, private schools that exist within poor communities but are claimed to be more effective than their public neighbours.[42] Such proposals differ from plans for "vouchers" proposed by neo-liberals, in that they aim to restrict eligibility to poor families, or give special treatment to the poor.[43] They have not so far been implemented in the United States, except in the unique and limited programme of vouchers for poor children in Milwaukee, described in Case Study 15 below. In Australia, on the other hand, where Catholic schools provide a subsidised local alternative available to many poorer families (see country summary), there is no evidence that they are more effective than public ones. It must be borne in mind that the existence of local private alternatives in poor areas of both the United States and Australia has more to do with historical, ethnic and religious factors than with any policies to extend school choice. This limits lessons for other countries.

Choice and educational costs

A final implication of school choice that cannot be ignored is its impact on educational costs. This may work in both directions.

On the one hand, choice can make education more expensive, where offering more educational options has costs attached. In some countries, it means providing more schools, whose smaller average size might reduce economies of scale. In the Netherlands, the government makes explicit the right to choose among schools of different religious or secular character in each community where there is sufficient demand. The minimum size requirement is low by international standards. The extra cost involved is considered politically acceptable, although it has recently been reduced by redefining the minimum size of school (see country summary). In Sweden, where private schools start up in small rural communities with no public school, the average cost of schooling in the municipality may rise. Support for smaller and more expensive schools are here implicitly recognised as a possible consequence of policy, rather than being a stated policy goal. In Denmark, small private schools are explicitly favoured with higher subsidies.

Choice through programme diversity can also cost money. Magnet schools in the United States and specialised schools elsewhere tend to get special funds for their programmes. New Zealand's Maori schools (see Case Study 10) do not, and suffer as a consequence, since they need to develop curriculum materials in a language that has never previously been taught through the written word.

On the other hand, policies associated with school choice are sometimes associated with public expenditure cuts. In particular, the devolution of budgetary responsibilities has been associated, for example in Sweden, New Zealand and England, with central governments wanting to pass to somebody else the difficult and unpopular decision of where to make economies. In 1991, Denmark introduced a masterful new system (described in Case Study 14) of giving money to private schools. The government makes the political decision of what is affordable, but the distribution of money is entirely in the hands of the schools and the market. There is nothing inherently wrong with the idea that some budgetary decisions can be made more effectively at school level, nor that imaginative and entrepreneurial school leaders can stretch limited public funds further than bureaucrats. But where new policies for devolution and "choice" are accompanied by too drastic cuts in public resources, the danger is that parents will associate them with a decline rather than improvement in the opportunities, choices and quality of schooling available.

Conclusion: in search of school markets that clear

In market theory, demand is matched with supply through adjustments in the quantity of goods on the market and their price. In education, most "buyers" (parents and children) are not subjected to a price constraint because their schooling is free, and most "sellers" (schools) are not in a position to vary the number of places supplied, except to a limited degree. At a system-wide level, supply of school places is in principle matched with pupil demand (which is highly predictable in a situation in which "consumption" is compulsory) through centralised planning. The need to find a place for every pupil and the pressure to avoid the waste of over-provision discourage governments from relinquishing much control over the supply of school places even when schools are chosen rather than allocated. This creates a problem to the extent that the distribution of school choices does not correspond to the distribution of school places. The market continues to clear at a system level: every pupil finds a school place, and vice versa. But in the market for places at a particular school now considered to be delivering a distinguishable "product", demand may exceed supply. The result is frustration.

Where politicians are unwilling to allow the number of school places to expand and contract freely with demand, the only way that this frustration will be avoided is if there is a relatively even spread of choices. One way this can happen is for the great majority of people to continue to choose an "assigned" school, with the threat of escape to others acting only as a discipline on the system. This is roughly the objective in Sweden. A very different model is to create a variety of attractive options that produce non-hierarchical choices of schools not based on residence. A "universal magnet" system can have this result; in Montclair, New Jersey, the majority of pupils do not attend their local school, yet 90 per cent have their first or second choice of school satisfied (see Case Study 9). Systems that are the furthest from either the Montclair or the Swedish model are those in which a strong hierarchy of schools has developed, with everybody wishing to attend the ones commonly judged as "best". While such judgements persist, school choice will continue to cause frustration, and may also intensify social divisions.

Chapter 4

Choice and the Cultural Context

Parents all over the world have similar concerns about their children's futures. Faced with uncertainty, particularly in terms of employment, many see education as having high stakes for their children, and are increasingly anxious to ensure that they attend a good school. This helps make school choice a universal theme.

But the reality of school choice depends to a large degree on local conditions. This is due not only to different educational structures and traditions, but also to social and cultural factors that determine how parents and pupils actually choose. There are therefore limits to the transferability of policy experiments. A system of choice widely considered politically unacceptable in one country may be politically unavoidable in another. An example is public subsidies for private religious schools in the United States and the Netherlands respectively. The country summaries in Part II illustrate some of these cultural differences. The following factors are particularly important.

The position of religion and the nature of pluralism

As discussed at the beginning of this report, the relationship between Church and State influenced the degree of choice of religious schooling accepted after the establishment of universal education systems. Such arrangements are rarely disturbed even in a more secular age, and when they are, it is usually to enhance the position of religious schools rather than diminish them. Australia's adoption of subsidies for private education in the 1970s saved a large but declining Catholic school sector. Many supporters of "private school choice" in the United States aim to do the same, and may be encouraged by the fact that Australia's constitutional exclusion of public support for a religion, identical to that in the United States, was interpreted by the courts as not applying to support for education in religious schools. But the United States lacks a further condition that has been a central ingredient in Australia, as in the Netherlands: a close association between a Church and a governing political party. In France, support for the Church in some sections of the right-of-centre majority elected in 1993 influenced the new government's plans to finance Catholic schools on a more favourable basis. However, a more powerful influence was the electoral advantage of promising greater opportunities to choose private religious schools, a choice that most French parents would like available, for not always religious reasons.

Today, the question of religious worship is a relatively minor aspect of pluralism in schools. In the United States, despite the still strong idea that public money should only be devoted to schools that are not just secular but "common" to all children, the diversity that is tolerated elsewhere in society breaks through in certain aspects of schooling. Compared to France, where even the Catholic private schools follow a well-defined national curriculum, differences both within and between American schools is considerable. The spread of "immersion" schools in foreign languages, the existence of "magnet schools", "academies" and "alternative schools" of every flavour, the wide range of private schools and the growth of home-schooling are all "exceptions" to a common school "norm" that illustrate a pluralistic ethos. A cosmopolitan heritage and a toleration of difference are national characteristics that encourage pluralistic school choice. In Denmark, though, toleration has permitted real educational choices despite a cultural homogeneity that limits to about 10 per cent the number who exercise it.

However, as countries become more cosmopolitan, they do not necessarily grow more educationally tolerant or educationally diverse. Economic and social turbulence has accompanied social change and ethnic diversification (through migration) in many OECD countries in recent years. A significant response both of individuals and of society as a whole has been to see education as responsible both for reformulating the basic values that bind a country together and for putting it back on a path to economic success. Concluding CERI's 1987 report on multicultural education, Professor Walo Hutmacher suggests "that a new universal culture has become the principal objective towards which the drive for homogenisation is being directed".[44] Hutmacher compares the influence of economic rationalism on education during the late 20th century with that of the late 19th century, when universal education was being proposed by the secular State. Today, pressure for a schooling that brings economic benefits comes not just from the State but in many cases from individuals, worried about the uncertainty of employment. In such an environment, true educational experimentation can be difficult even in the most tolerant of settings. Even in Denmark, for example, some of the more radical school movements established in the 1960s have been brought more down to earth by the concerns of the 1990s' parents (see Case Study 14).

Perceptions of educational quality

The case for school choice has sometimes been presented more forcefully in countries where a significant proportion of public schools are perceived to be failing than in countries where a consistent quality is thought to be maintained across the school system. In the United States and the United Kingdom, for example, the sight of some better-off families "escaping" less desired public schools by selecting a neighbourhood or paying for private education has raised the question of why everyone should not be able to make such a choice. This question has not arisen in Sweden, where quality is perceived to be more even, and the opportunity of school choice has only been taken up by a small minority.

International comparison of reading scores indicates that school differences account for far more variation in pupil performance in some countries than in others. Figure 1 shows the percentage of variance in 14 year-olds' scores associated with school differences. In the Nordic countries, such school variations are extremely low; in New Zealand, the United States and Ireland they are high, even though schools for 14 year-olds supposedly cater for pupils of all abilities. In the Netherlands, as in Germany and Switzerland, inter-school variations are unsurprising, since pupils are divided between

Figure 1
Disaggregation of variance in the reading achievement scores of 14 year-olds into between-school and within-school components (1991)

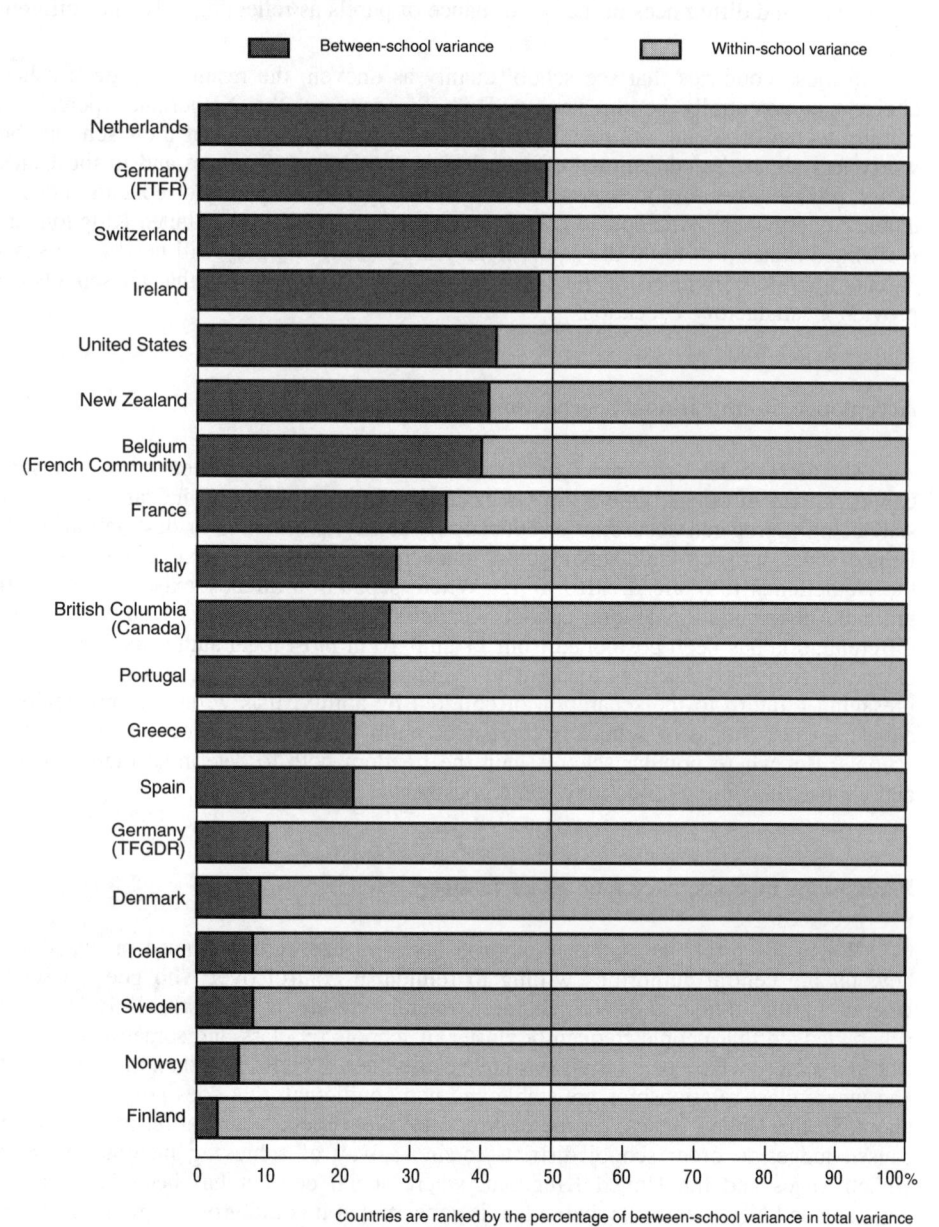

Country	Between-school variance (%)
Netherlands	~50
Germany (FTFR)	~49
Switzerland	~48
Ireland	~47
United States	~43
New Zealand	~42
Belgium (French Community)	~40
France	~35
Italy	~28
British Columbia (Canada)	~27
Portugal	~26
Greece	~22
Spain	~21
Germany (TFGDR)	~10
Denmark	~9
Iceland	~8
Sweden	~8
Norway	~5
Finland	~3

Countries are ranked by the percentage of between-school variance in total variance

Note: This indicator, from *Education at a Glance*, OECD (1993), is based on data collected for the IEA study of reading performance of 14 year-olds in the 1991 school year. It presents the variation that is accounted for by differences between schools as a per cent of total variation in student reading performance.

lower secondary schools broadly according to their abilities. So whereas Americans and New Zealanders worry that differences in school quality may create a polarisation of opportunity along broadly social lines, the Dutch tend to regard school quality as relatively even, and differences in the performance of pupils as reflecting only their different abilities.

In those countries that see school quality as uneven, the results of greater school choice can potentially be threatening. Both Sweden and the Netherlands perceive a certain degree of social and racial polarisation occurring in some of their schools, but worry less about the educational effects than in the United Kingdom and in the United States, precisely because it is assumed that a broadly similar quality of education can be attained everywhere. Attempts to create "national standards" in the United Kingdom and the United States aim to do the same. If they are to succeed, they will need to persuade parents hitherto convinced of the importance of school differences that all schools can provide a satisfactory education.

Acceptance of educational segregation

The ideal of the "common" or "comprehensive" school has been stronger in some countries than in others. One issue has been at what age pupils of the same age group start being segregated according to educational ability, preference or destination. In the United States, most children stay together in a common high school until the age of 18; in the Netherlands they are divided at 12. Where separation already exists on scholastic grounds, differentiation among schools becomes less of an issue. In England, where differentiation has been postponed from 11 until 16 in most local authorities, the idea of choice is frequently seen as a threat to "comprehensive" secondary schools, and as presaging a return to the separation of children by ability. It is wrong automatically to equate greater choice of school by parent or pupil with greater selection of pupils by schools. But where popular schools gain the freedom both to determine their character and choose their pupils, this may sometimes be the result.

Perceptions of class, race and social justice

Where the principle of the common school has been compromised or abandoned, how far are central authorities willing to relinquish control over who goes to school where? In the Netherlands, a genuinely liberal attitude is maintained. It is widely acknowledged that people frequently cluster in schools by class and sometimes by race. But in a society where racial divisions have caused less social unrest than in many others, and where class relationships are stable and non-conflictual, this does not cause general alarm. In the United States, on the contrary, *de facto* racial segregation in schools has caused judges to order school districts to find a way of achieving integration. In the United States and the United Kingdom, where social conflict has been high, and in Australia and New Zealand, where there is concern that it could grow, there are fears that uncontrolled choice might intensify social polarisation. These anxieties may in some cases limit the scope of choice policies; another possibility is to design the policy directly as an instrument of social justice. America's "magnet" schools have used a controlled form of choice to pursue desegregation. Milwaukee's voucher scheme (Case Study 15) is restricted to the poor. England's city technology colleges (Case Study 7) must accept a socially balanced intake in inner city areas. New Zealand's support for *Kura Kaupapa Maori (Case Study 10)* is to some extent an effort to meet the needs of a socially and culturally marginalised group. These examples are more the exception than the norm, but illustrate how choice can be skewed to a country's social concerns.

Geographical patterns and school size

Only in densely-populated cities is choice among a range of schools normally feasible. For a Swede or an Australian living in a small settlement 100 kilometres from the next town, the only issue is whether the choice of a single school is provided locally. In Denmark, the Netherlands and Sweden, "choice" policies have in many cases allowed small communities to choose to start a private school at public expense where the municipality has not provided one. In urban as well as in rural areas, the minimum size of school tolerated by the government has a critical effect on choices available. In both Haarlem and East Harlem – the Netherlands and New York[45] – urban children have a wide choice because schools are small by international standards. Small schools are potentially expensive, although in East Harlem economies are made by siting more than one school in a building and avoiding the cost of counselling services required in larger, more impersonal, environments. Insofar as costs are higher, their acceptability depends on local and national political priorities.

The development of relationships between central government, local government and schools

School choice is closely associated with the autonomy of schools to manage their own destiny, to define a separate character and to compete with other schools for pupils. There is a common trend towards devolution to schools in OECD countries, but from many different institutional backgrounds.

The relationship between decision-making at various levels varies greatly, as shown in Figure 2.

Both New Zealand and Sweden have devolved most decisions from centralised to local decision-making. But whereas in New Zealand, with no local education authorities, 73 per cent of decisions are now taken by schools, Sweden's municipalities have retained half of all decisions. They control, for example, the proportion of school budgets that is based on student enrolments. In the United States an unparalleled amount of decision-making at the very local school district level prevents schools from having much of a say over their own destiny. This situation has been widely criticised. Although Chubb and Moe's[46] radical proposal to shift decision-making almost entirely to the school level is unlikely to be adopted, it has opened a new debate about how to stimulate initiative at the school level.

These country examples point to the common conclusion that schools and local education authorities compete for power over decision-making. School-based decision-making is not identical to school choice: some American school districts, for example, have instigated and supervise systems attempting to maximise choice of school for every

Figure 2
Locus of decision-making in lower secondary education (1991)

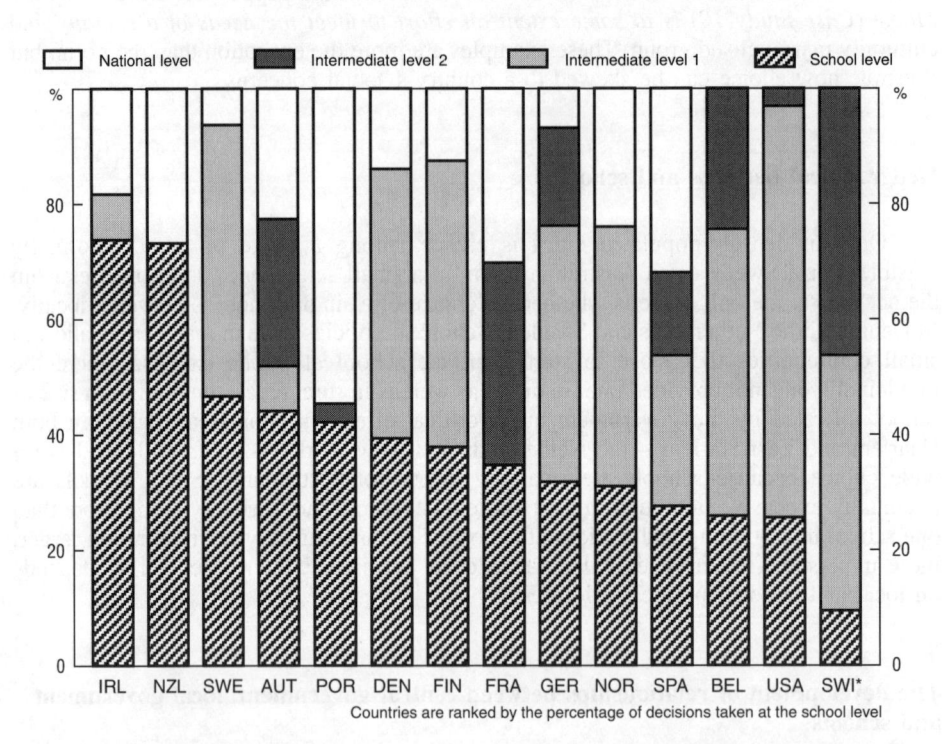

☐ National level ■ Intermediate level 2 ☐ Intermediate level 1 ▨ School level

IRL NZL SWE AUT POR DEN FIN FRA GER NOR SPA BEL USA SWI*
Countries are ranked by the percentage of decisions taken at the school level

Note: This indicator is based on decisions in four areas: educational planning and structures, personnel management, organisation of instruction, and resources. Any results are dependent on the list of decisions that were selected for inclusion in each category and must be interpreted within this context.
The decision-making levels – the locations where these decisions are taken – are as follows:
1. The institution and/or school.
2. Intermediate 1 (closest to the school).
3. Intermediate 2 (often regional level).
4. Country (central government).

Decisions taken at these levels include only the primary decision-makers and do not include a measure of whether other decision-making levels are consulted during the decision-making process or whether decisions are taken within a framework stipulated by another decision-making level.

* The countries are, in this order, Ireland, New Zealand, Sweden, Austria, Portugal, Denmark, Finland, France, Germany, Norway, Spain, Belgium, the United States and Switzerland.

Source: OECD (1993), *Education at a Glance,* Paris.

pupil. But whether choice is based on such planning, or whether it is shaped by the decisions of autonomous and self-defining schools, will depend in many cases on the degree to which local authorities relinquish control.

Chapter 5

Conclusion and Recommendations: Aligning Choice Policies with Educational Objectives

It is not in the scope of this report to conclude whether greater choice of school is a good or a bad thing. But three broad conclusions have emerged from the study. First, that no school system can ignore completely the growing desire of parents and pupils to make choices that affect their educational opportunities. Selecting one's school is not the only such choice, but is often seen as critically important. Second, that policies to promote school choice can have a serious impact, sometimes undesired, on education systems and on educational chances. And third, that instruments are available to manage choice more effectively in line with desired educational and social outcomes. Although such management of school choice may appear to contradict the *laissez-faire* goals of some of its advocates, no government has in reality felt able to desist completely from planning publicly-financed education. This chapter identifies, in the form of recommendations, areas where intervention should be considered. But first it considers briefly the three conclusions mentioned above.

The degree to which school choice is a real aspiration for individuals rather than merely an issue invented by politicians is demonstrated by the way choices are made in practice. In a country like Sweden, where the possibility of attending a school other than the closest one is new, it is exercised far more rarely than in the Netherlands, where it is well established. What is perhaps more relevant than the amount of choice is the motivation behind it. The Dutch once chose schools almost purely on religious grounds; now perceptions of educational quality are becoming more important. In many countries, the idea of going to one's local school as the institution that will deliver a standard educational product is being widely questioned. True, most parents and pupils still prefer the closest school, but they make more demands on it than in the past; parents, who are on average more educated than they have ever been, perceive themselves increasingly as consumers. In such circumstances, a formal denial of the right of "exit" within the public system causes dissatisfied parents with the means to do so to find other ways of choosing. They may pay to use the private sector, move house to a neighbourhood with a more desired school or find some informal means of changing a school allocation.

But there is no automatic link between any one policy to extend school choice and the expansion of educational opportunities, nor between choice policies and the other objectives identified in Chapter 1. Opportunities may be limited not just by enrolment rules but by the number of places in various schools, by the amount of information about them available to pupils and parents and their closeness to people's homes. The second objective, to create competition to improve school performance, only exists to the extent that choices are made on the basis of comparisons of their effectiveness, which even professional educational researchers can spend years trying to assess. The third objective, to give parents' values greater influence in education, is commonly achieved by choice that creates new competition for enrolments, but may potentially conflict with certain other societal goals. Finally, allowing a free choice of school might potentially stimulate greater educational variety, but there is no evidence to show that it will necessarily do so.

At the same time, it is possible for school choice to have unintended consequences. When popular schools fill up, they become better resourced and more popular; when less desired schools lose pupils, they decline. The polarisation of school quality that may ensue is undesirable in itself, and more so where pupils who already have advantages end up in the best schools. Where choice creates hierarchy rather than variety in school provision, there are bound to be winners and losers.

None of these potential shortcomings can be fully "designed out" of a school-choice policy, whose outcomes will by definition be determined by the unpredictable preferences and decisions of many individuals. But care in the formulation of policies might both enhance policy effectiveness and limit the potential for unintended consequences. A first step is to recognise that no matter how much autonomy schools are granted, governments retain ultimate responsibility for the outcomes of school systems, as long as they use tax revenues to support them. That is why the most radical reforms described in this study stop short of giving schools full control of their capital resources, and thereby allow governments to continue to structure school provision. An important consequence of this is that the supply of places at popular schools is limited, and not all parents and pupils get the choices they desire. That in turn increases the duty on central or local school authorities to pursue an even distribution of educational opportunities.

Recommendations

The decision of whether to adopt particular policies to expand school choice will ultimately be taken in the political, institutional and cultural context of individual countries. But this study's findings suggest that education authorities consider the following measures to ensure that any such policies are well aligned with educational and other objectives:

- *Intervention to create choices for educationally underserved groups*

Creating the possibility of enrolment in a school other than the nearest public one is frequently not enough, on its own, to offer real choices to the educationally disadvantaged. A number of constraints may remain, including difficulties in obtaining information about other schools, in travelling to them or in being accepted on their rolls.

Public authorities can perform a significant function in providing better information about schools, which otherwise tends to be available through informal sources not equally obtainable by all parents and pupils. Any published indicators of performance should be as varied as possible, and avoid single measures that rank schools' output with no reference to the quality of their intake. Excessive reliance on self-presentation by individual schools may also be undesirable, and the possibility of parent-information centres providing neutral guidance merits attention.

School-transport policy should also be reconsidered in the light of choice. The desirability of presenting a range of school choices to each pupil needs, however, to be weighed against cost, environmental and traffic considerations. But a more crucial geographical constraint may be exclusion from popular schools that give priority to local residents. Where this systematically gives superior opportunities to children whose parents can afford to live near good schools, rules reserving some places for disadvantaged children regardless of residence should be considered.

- *Active diversification of educational supply*

Demand-led choice does not on its own tend to create educational pluralism: schools subject to open enrolment are more likely to compete at the margin for extra pupils than to redefine their character to serve a "niche" market. So where a wide choice of educational options is seen as desirable, a systematic initiative from educational providers is generally needed. Educational diversity may involve a range of approaches to schooling without necessarily requiring a high degree of pupil specialisation.

There are two big potential advantages of systematically combining choice with diversity. The first is that it might create a more even distribution of choices than the hierarchies that tend to emerge when all schools compete to deliver the same thing – and thus it will be possible to satisfy more choices. Secondly, there is a greater chance that educational innovation will result under a diversified than a hierarchical system of choice, and therefore more likelihood that choice will lead to improvements in education. However, the need to stimulate diversity on a system level creates the danger that schools will be assigned labels (such as "technology school") that are not genuinely reflected in a change of ethos. A balance between central stimulation and local entrepreneurship by educators therefore needs to be found.

- *Measures to improve the supply of chosen options*

The biggest frustration to parents and pupils is to be promised free choice of school, only to find that the most attractive schools are full. Where big differences in popularity exist, governments that have promised choice need to address this problem. One way is to intervene in less popular schools to help replicate the qualities sought by parents in successful ones. Another is to help successful schools to expand. This is likely to be feasible in a number of countries with expanding school rolls in the coming years. Governments that have claimed to increase school choice should use demand signals as a direct guide to such expansion, rather than relying purely on their own judgments of where new buildings should be sited. The case for allowing a team from a successful school to start another one nearby should be considered.

In this context, governments that give support to private schools should consider whether all sectors are being given an equal opportunity to respond to demand. It would be unfortunate if public money for teachers flowed to private schools that had the flexibility to build more classrooms, while popular public schools were turning children away because they lacked access to capital.

- *Clear criteria for schools' choice of pupils*

In the many cases where demand for a school exceeds supply, the fact that schools will need to select pupils must be openly accepted; and the criteria on which selection is made should be openly debated. The alternative is a pretence that all schools are open to everyone, accompanied by vague or unpopular criteria for selection. Insofar as selection is made by residence, the limits to "open" enrolment outside one's catchment area need to be made clear to parents. If some schools select children according to ability, the consequences for all schools needs to be considered, since opportunities in schools that lose their more clever pupils might well be affected. In general, a system that allows every school to define its own clientele will change the structure of schooling in a manner unlikely to ensure the greatest possible choice for the greatest number.

Part II
COUNTRY SUMMARIES

Australia
Twenty years of subsidy for private schools

Introduction

Since 1973, the federal (Commonwealth) government of Australia has provided subsidies to all private (non-government) schools. A matching subsidy of varying amounts has been provided by each of Australia's six states. This summary focuses on the choice between public and private schools supported by these subsidies. A full picture of school choice in Australia would also require an examination of choice among public schools in the various states, which is not attempted here. An example of a policy to extend choice within one state, New South Wales, is described in Case Study 6. But the public-private choice is more significant in Australia than in most countries because of the size of the private sector, which accounted for 28 per cent of enrolments in 1991.

Support for private schools was designed chiefly to maintain an already large school sector in financial difficulty, and to raise standards in that sector. The subsidy is therefore distributed in inverse proportion to the private resources of the school. But every school gets some public money, and private enrolments have grown steadily, from 21 per cent of the total in 1971. This raises wider issues than the continuation of existing under-resourced schools. True, 70 per cent of private schools are Catholic, mostly charging low fees and serving a stable population of mixed social origin. But recent growth has been primarily in non-Catholic schools, which on average cater for children from more privileged backgrounds. Critics fear a trend towards polarisation in opportunities as independent schools continue to grow, and as their growth affects the quality of public schools. But the principle of subsidy to private schools is well established and politically inviolable in the foreseeable future.

Main characteristics

The rules governing subsidy, which have been changed several times over the past 20 years, at present work as follows. Schools are divided into twelve bands on the basis of "need", linked to their private resources from fees and donations. Each school receives a recurrent grant for each of its pupils from the federal government. This grant equals a percentage of the average cost of educating a pupil in Australia's public schools, ranging from 12 to 49 per cent according to which band the school is in. This is topped up by a grant from the state government of between 20 and 25 per cent of average pupil cost.

Thus a poor school in a high "band" whose costs are lower than the public average can come close to total government funding, while a private school charging a high fee and spending more than average per pupil recoups only a small proportion from government. Catholic schools, educating 70 per cent of private school pupils in 1991, all come into band 10, the third most generous. The reason is that all schools run as a single private school "system" get equal funding, and fees in Catholic schools are only a fifth as high as in other private schools (see Table 1). In the Catholic system, 72 per cent of 1991 income came from public grants.

Table 1. **Private schooling in Australia**

	Catholic schools	Other private ("independent")
Number of schools (1991)	1 691	758
Number of enrolments (1991)	601 460	259 824
Share of total school enrolment (%):		
– 1981	17.9	5.1
– 1986	19.4	7.1
– 1991	19.5	8.4
Average fee (A$, 1991):		
– Primary	349	1 434
– Secondary	1 014	3 293
– Combined	1 288	3 892
– All	691	3 501

Source: Department of Employment, Education and Training.

Most of the non-Catholic private schools adhere to other religions; the biggest are Anglican, Uniting Church and Lutheran. However, while most Catholic schools draw the great majority of their pupils from local Catholic communities, most frequently of Irish descent, many other private schools draw pupils more widely and distinguish themselves first by a high academic reputation and only secondly by a broadly Christian setting. Most are run as individual organisations rather than as multi-school systems. This helps explain why the non-Catholic private schools are referred to as the "independent" sector.

Since 1986, the New Schools Policy has governed the conditions under which new non-government schools will be supported, in terms of capital as well as recurrent funding. Committees in each state and territory make recommendations attempting to reconcile planning and efficiency with choice and diversity. They aim to ensure a balance of public and private provision in each area, and to avoid simple substitution of non-government for government schools. The New Schools Policy also limits the resources for smaller start-up schools, by placing all new schools not in a "system" in the less generous six funding bands.

History and politics

The introduction of subsidies for private schools by a Labour government in 1973 had an educational rationale but a political motive. Both were linked to a crisis for Catholic schools, which had long provided education to a substantial section of the population, largely of low and middle incomes. The crisis was precipitated by the reduction of the number of monks and nuns serving as unpaid teachers in schools, following changes in the Church after the Second Vatican Council. This threatened the financial viability of schools charging very low fees, which could survive only with classes of up to 60 pupils. The educational rationale for subsidy was to improve standards in these schools. The political motive, linked to an election, was to deliver the Catholic vote, closely associated with Labour.

Australia's Constitution forbids public support for a religion. In the late 1970s it was established definitively in court that this did not exclude support for a child's education in a private school that happened to have a religious identity. But it would have been impossible to finance only Catholic schools, even though their rescue was the object of the original policy. Labour has therefore tolerated public subsidy to all private schools, even though philosophically it distinguishes between the Catholic system's commitment to provide for children regardless of parental income, and the existence of independent schools catering largely for an upper-middle-class élite. However, the conjunction of Labour commitment to Catholic schools and right-of-centre parties' support for all private schools makes the existence of subsidies for private education politically stable. This does not prevent constant change in the terms of the subsidies. During the 1980s, Labour created a banding system highly favourable to the Catholics, and through the New Schools Policy made it harder for new small schools with scarce resources, notably "fundamentalist" Christian schools, to get started. Labour's political opponents proposed a policy at the 1993 election (won by Labour) that would have reduced the number of needs bands and substantially increased funding to the independent sector.

Choice patterns in practice

Longitudinal research in the Australian context[47] suggests that the socio-economic advantages of upper-middle-class origins repeat their effects in terms of secondary school choice. Over 90 per cent of a sample of parents who had attended independent schools planned to make the same choice for their children. This is linked by researchers to the presumption of private schooling as an investment that yields tangible returns.[48] But choice of Catholic schools seems to be related largely to religious identity and family traditions of attending such schools, especially among boys.[49] This choice appears to cut across social origins and early career attainments.

This evidence implies that many Australians consider schools only in one sector, and that choice between public and private schools is not necessarily an active process. However, recent growth in the proportion of enrolments at independent schools indicates that not all families choose according to their own history. Case Study 5 on Melbourne confirms that direct competition between public and private (especially Catholic) schools has been limited. But it points to a possible increase in such competition, especially between the best-regarded public schools and independent schools, in a state that is devolving responsibilities to its public schools and encouraging them to become more entrepreneurial. It should also be noted that in the transition from primary to secondary school, there has since the 1970s been a substantial net switch in favour of the private sector, with the public sector losing about 8 per cent of its pupils.

Examples of impact

The existence of public subsidies has undoubtedly helped Australian private schools to survive and grow, and for Catholic schools in particular to improve their educational content through better resourcing. Not all of that growth can be attributed to subsidy arrangements, however. During the late 1980s, prosperity contributed to a rise in independent enrolments while the Catholic share remained constant (see Table 1), despite a concentration of subsidies on Catholic schools. That growth was checked by the recession of the early 1990s.

Does the subsidy have an impact on private school affordability and thus access to private schooling? The evidence is mixed. The average school fee fell by over half between 1972 and 1982 but rose again by over 20 per cent in the following decade. It may be that this represented a one-off fall in the price of Catholic schooling, which secured a private option for a group of relatively modest means, followed by an expansion of the more expensive independent school market as the number of better-off families grew.

This has led to considerable concern that after the "rescuing" of Catholic schools, the further expansion of the private sector creates mainly choices for the privileged. The large size of this sector, and its rapid growth in comparison to private school sectors in other OECD countries, is argued to pose a serious threat to the public school sector. Analysis, by Don Anderson of the Australian National University, of 1976 and 1986 census data shows that the shift to private education has been highest among residents of particular privileged suburbs as well as among members of certain occupational groups. "If present trends continue", Anderson warns, "the function of public schooling will become primarily that of a safety net for the residue of children not catered for by the private sector".[50]

The figures in Table 2 indicate that this situation on a national scale may still be some way off. Although the independent sector clearly caters mainly for more privileged groups, the public sector is not yet a social ghetto. Professional and managerial workers

Table 2. **Father's occupation and type of school (%)**

	Public school	Catholic school	Other private school
Professional and managerial	21	34	64
Small business and clerical	21	24	18
Craft workers	25	17	11
Manual and service workers	34	25	7
Total	100	100	100

Source: D. Anderson (1992), "The interaction of public and private school systems", *Australian Journal of Education*, p. 225.

constitute about one-quarter of the workforce, and while they are greatly over-represented in independent schools, they are far from absent in public ones. As Anderson points out, however, polarisation is much greater in certain areas, including one suburb (Hawthorn in Melbourne) where 57 per cent of secondary school children attended private schools in 1986.

Conclusion: choice in the Australian setting

Public support for the choice of private schools has been introduced to uphold a form of pluralism that has always existed in Australia. The Catholic community is heavily concentrated geographically, and has been able to retain its own schools without causing major problems for the education system as a whole. However, the main effect of recent public financial support for this system has not been to spread educational pluralism to include new groups (few new migrants from Asia or Southeast Europe have set up schools), but to extend choice of private school for educational rather than cultural or religious reasons. Independent schools potentially create a more varied educational setting, divert more money into schooling and produce more centres of educational excellence. But the beneficiaries are those who can afford the average A$ 3 500 a year charged in the independent sector. For some observers of this situation, the relatively small amount of subsidy that goes to independent schools is simply the political price of sustaining a Catholic school choice. For others, the steady growth, with public assistance, of a sector that caters for a privileged minority poses a threat to the stability of the whole education system.

England[51]

Creating a public-sector market for schools

Introduction

The British government puts school choice and the role of consumers at the centre of its declared policies for education. In 1991 it formulated a "Parents' Charter" to underpin this philosophy. Its policies aim to open up schools to market pressures, by allowing parents greater freedom to select schools within the public sector, by giving them more information to help them make this choice, by directing resources to schools according to how many pupils enrol and by permitting greater variety in the types of school available. Unlike some countries, its efforts to improve choice have been directed primarily at the public sector rather than involving general financial support for private schools.

There is no doubt that open enrolment and pupil-based funding policies, along with policies devolving management to schools, have indeed created a more competitive environment, with parents choosing more actively and schools trying harder to attract pupils. Advocates point to the energising effect this has had on some schools; critics point to evidence of social polarisation and to the possibility of selection of pupils by popular schools if they are over-subscribed.

But the other main strand of government choice policy, the encouragement of diversity, has yet to create a decisive transformation. Critics, including some strong supporters of choice, question whether true diversity can exist within the framework of England's new national curriculum. The creation of a new sector of schools, maintained directly by central government grants rather than controlled by local education authorities, has not obviously increased diversity from the point of view of the consumer.

A new strand of policy aims to stimulate diversity by encouraging specialisation. But future patterns of school choice in England will depend on the criteria by which schools are judged. Will parents choose according to schools' general qualities – including ability to deliver a standard educational product defined by the national curriculum? Or will they select according to schools' special features – such as distinctive educational ideas or extra subject specialisms? By mid-1993, five years after the first broad legislation associated with school choice, the first of these criteria – and hence the competitive rather than the pluralistic model of choice – was clearly prevalent.

Main characteristics

Until the 1980s, school admission rules in England were set by local education authorities – elected local government bodies that had responsibility for all publicly-funded schools. Each authority determined both the intake level of every school and whether pupils had to attend the school in their catchment area or were given a wider choice. Some local authorities retained grammar schools which selected by ability; some offered a choice between single-sex and mixed schools. About 20 per cent of schools were "voluntary-aided" – mainly funded by local authorities but partly controlled by foundations (religious as a rule), which appoint a majority of members of the governing boards that control admission policies.

Central government has superimposed a number of changes on this system. Their aim with respect to choice is twofold: to improve choices within the local authority sector and to create more choices outside it.

Choice has been promoted within local authority schools by:
- *Opening up enrolment rules.* Any child may apply to any school, and may not be refused unless it is over-subscribed, except in cases of selective schools and church schools. The capacity of a school is set partly in relation to its enrolment level of 1979, when the school-age population was high. Where demand exceeds capacity, local authorities continue to determine in most cases the rules for admitting pupils. Legislation effectively allows parents to express a preference of school, but does not guarantee that the preference will be met.
- *Linking school funding more closely to enrolments.* This is made possible by requiring local authorities to devolve financial management to schools. At least 90 per cent of their schooling expenditure must be delegated to the governing bodies that control individual schools; at least 80 per cent of this school budget must be determined by the number of pupils enrolled.

The local authority "monopoly" on publicly-funded schooling has been broken by:
- *Allowing schools to opt out of local authority control.* A school may apply to be maintained by a direct grant from central government, following a ballot of parents. "Grant-maintained" schools enjoy more autonomy than local authority ones; for example, they may determine their own admission arrangements subject to the agreement of the Secretary of State for Education. By mid-1993, there were some 500 grant-maintained schools, mainly secondary schools, of which there are 3 500 in England. About 400 more had voted to apply for grant-maintained status.
- *The creation of "city technology colleges" (CTCs).* These specialist secondary schools operate as independent organisations, with running costs paid by central government and start-up capital shared between government and business sponsors. Based mainly in inner-city areas, they draw students from a wide area and innovate in science and technology, with particular emphasis on using information technology, within the national curriculum. By 1993, 15 CTCs were operating.
- *Public support for poor pupils to attend private schools.* The Assisted Places Scheme, introduced in 1981, helps able children from lower-income families to pay school fees. By 1993, some 28 000 pupils were being helped in this way.

Finally, it should be noted that the government promotes consumer information about schools across sectors. It has introduced:

- *A new system of school inspection.* Each school is formally inspected every four years in a common framework, and reports are made available to parents. This applies to all publicly-funded schools, including CTCs, but not to private schools.
- *A requirement for schools to provide better performance information to parents, and to provide test and exam results to the government for publication.* Although private schools are exempt, their results have been included in the "school performance tables" published annually for each local authority since 1992.

History and politics

The history of school choice policies since the election of the Conservative government in 1979 has been closely bound up with the evolving relationship between central government, local government, schools and parents. An important tenet of the central administration has been that local authorities have paid too much attention to the dictums of education "professionals" and not enough to parents' views when running schools. In attempting to change this, the government has increased the power of: parents as consumers – by enabling them to "vote with their feet" for schools; parents as producers – by giving them a greater say on school governing boards; and schools as producers – by giving them power previously held by local authorities, with the ultimate power to opt out altogether.

From 1980, local authorities were required to take parental preferences into account when allocating school places, but were still allowed to manage them in line with their own planning priorities. This limited measure to allow more open enrolment survived until the sweeping Education Reform Act of 1988, which was influenced by trends in the intervening period.

The 1980s were years of sharply falling school rolls, due to low birth rates during the second half of the 1970s. Local authorities were accused of putting an artificial lid on enrolment numbers in some schools in order to keep others viable, thus allowing planning rather than market forces to determine which schools survived. So the 1988 Act introduced the rule preventing enrolments from being kept below the school's theoretical capacity. Another central government perception during the 1980s was that some Labour-controlled local authorities were forcing ideologically-motivated policies on schools against the wishes of parents. The 1988 Act therefore introduced grant-maintained schools, which were initially envisaged as an escape route from local government control rather than a means of becoming something different. The 1988 Act also included provisions for the setting up of CTCs, for local management of schools and for a national curriculum and testing system.

In the following five years, the biggest issue to emerge was the shape and purpose of the grant-maintained sector. Politically, attention focused on the various incentives offered by the government to schools to encourage them to "opt out", and on the role of a new central Funding Agency which from April 1994 has responsibility for funding these schools. Educationally, the most interesting development has been the degree to which grant-maintained schools change their identity. In a 1992 White Paper, *Choice and Diversity,* the Department of Education portrayed grant-maintained schools as allowing "substantially increased diversity", and encouraged all schools to develop their strengths. It also created a provision for new grant-maintained "technology colleges" similar to CTCs. The relaxation of rules under which grant-maintained schools can apply for a change of character has raised the politically-charged issue of a possible return to grammar schools, which select on ability. The government, which must approve changes of character, stated in the White Paper that it did not intend "either to encourage or to discourage such applications", but would consider each on its merits in relation to the local context.

Choice patterns in practice

There is now considerable evidence of the way parents choose schools under open enrolment in England (as well as in Scotland, where it has existed for longer).[52] Various studies do not point to any single pattern, but some common elements emerge. Location is clearly important, with a large proportion of parents opting for their nearest school unless there is a specific reason not to do so. Yet there is a considerable amount of active choice, from all social classes – although various studies appear to show differing tendencies in terms of how different classes choose. One survey[53] suggests that working-class families tend to look for an environment in which their children feel comfortable, while for middle-class parents the overriding factor is an environment characterised by academic success. This research is consistent with detailed analysis of the choice process being carried out by Stephen Ball and others at King's College, London. Their work[54] shows that children's preferences, while important generally in choosing secondary schools, are more decisive in working-class families, and that middle-class parents are more likely to influence their children into sharing their own value judgements about schools.

One thing that is conspicuously lacking in such surveys is any evidence that parents choose according to schools' special educational features – as opposed to their atmosphere, academic qualities or closeness. Evidence on schools' marketing behaviour would confirm that they would not like to portray themselves as serving a particular *niche*. The King's College researchers found remarkable similarity in head teachers' speeches to prospective parents at open evenings, and a tendency to balance every special feature with a countervailing one: if a school was "strong on special needs", its ability to cater for gifted children would also be stressed; if "strong on technology", a description of its fine arts strengths would follow. Even at city technology colleges, which are specialised by definition, heads are keen to emphasize other subject strengths as well.

The popularity of CTCs (in school year 1991 the ratio of applicants to places ranged from 4.4 to 1.8) may illustrate not that English parents are looking for schools that are *specialised*, but that they are easily attracted to schools seen as *special*. The CTCs pull pupils from a wide geographical area; unlike some other nationalities, the English are used to the concept that routes to educational success may lie in centres of academic excellence rather than comprehensive neighbourhood schools. "Public schools" (*i.e.* élite private boarding schools) have for centuries educated the country's ruling class; from the 1940s until the 1970s, grammar schools were seen as an alternative route to academic success open to bright children from all classes. Today, not just CTCs but also some grant-maintained schools seem to be benefiting from the image of being different and therefore special in terms of academic excellence. The Grant Maintained Schools Centre reported in 1991 that the majority of schools had experienced an increase in rolls (on average 5.3 per cent) after opting out.

Examples of impact

Three key questions might be asked about the impact of school choice in England. Is it changing schools' behaviour? Does it affect their educational performance? And does it affect the distribution of educational opportunities?

To the first question, the answer is certainly yes. Schools have become much more aware of their client group, done more to woo and inform them, and attempted to improve their appeal. There is no formal evidence to measure such changes, but some are obvious to any observer. Open evenings, brochures and public relations generally have been handled with greater care and professionalism than in the past. In the effort to "smarten" their image, a large number of schools have adopted school uniforms or dress codes. These efforts seem more often to attempt to portray an image of high moral and academic standards than one of intellectual excitement.

Any effects on schools' educational performance is harder to pin down. An inspectorate report on grant-maintained schools in 1993[55] found that the quality of teaching was not significantly worse or better than in local authority schools, and that improvements in results were in line with general trends. Since open enrolment was introduced at the same time as the national curriculum, it will be hard ever to separate out its impact. One important trend to watch, however, will be the relationship between school inspection and improvement in performance. Anecdotal evidence suggests that under the new system in which inspection reports may make or break a school's reputation, schools are preparing for inspections months in advance – potentially with more than superficial improvements.

But the most emotive question regarding the impact of school choice is its effect on educational opportunities. Since popular schools are not automatically given capital resources to expand, the promise of school choice has led to much disappointment – when pupils are turned away because schools are full. In 30 local authorities surveyed in the autumn of 1992, the number of appeals were rising; in only two were they falling.[56]

Since the most common means of selecting pupils in over-subscribed schools is by residence, living close to a popular school remains the easiest way to get in. There is a danger that under such a system, schools will become more polarised in terms of reputation and social class of their intake. While local reports of such effects abound, this is not easy to measure on a system-wide level. The King's College research cited above identifies a tendency of middle-class parents in London to choose schools in which parents are of the same social class.[57] Any tendency to cluster may potentially work against opportunities for pupils from working-class families, by concentrating socially-disadvantaged children. In contrast, city technology colleges give opportunities to a small number of children consciously selected from a wide range of abilities and social and geographical settings.

Conclusion: choice in the English setting

Perhaps the biggest problem with school choice in England is the national habit of ranking educational alternatives rather than seeing them as being of possibly equal value. This potentially makes school choice an exercise in which for every winner there is a loser. The pluralistic attitude to education evident in the Netherlands and Denmark, and in some contexts in the United States, seems unlikely to take root easily in England.

Although there may be many exceptions to this picture, as there are to English class attitudes generally, the existing terms of public debate do not help. The obsession of the press in highlighting the country's "best" schools after the publication of the first "league tables" of examination results in 1992 is the most obvious illustration.

But if England has less chance than most countries of achieving educational diversity through choice, it has certainly gone further than most in bringing consumers into the process of educational change. In a fierce debate over the testing of schoolchildren during the Spring of 1993, parents at the school gates were heard hotly debating the merits of diagnostic versus summative testing. This new engagement, for all the controversy and bitterness that have been generated in England's school choice debate, may yet create a new dynamic that helps to make schooling more effective.

The Netherlands
Equal treatment for public and private schools

Introduction

The Netherlands is exceptional among OECD countries in that it finances public and private schools on a completely equal basis. This situation was created by a historical settlement between secular and religious interests at the beginning of the 20th century. Today, some two-thirds of all primary and secondary pupils are enrolled in privately-governed schools, the great majority of them either Protestant or Catholic and the rest mainly non-religious. Given the central government's direct financing of these schools' expenditure on the same basis as those governed by municipalities, they are not as independent as private schools in most other countries. But for convenience, and because there is no financially independent sector in the Netherlands, they are referred to here as "private".

These arrangements were set up in the Netherlands to guarantee a certain kind of school choice: the choice to attend a school adhering to one's preferred religious or secular "world view" (*richting*). The State has agreed to finance the establishment or continuation of a school for each religion or belief system wherever a local demand can be demonstrated. Until relatively recently, this has not in practice involved active choices among schools for most parents or pupils. Dutch society was highly "pillarised" into Protestant, Catholic and secular groups, and the decision of which local school to go to, according to which pillar one belongs to, was self-evident. However, in the past two or three decades, these pillars have become far weaker, and more people have started to choose actively between schools in different sectors.

The resulting "shift from a religious-based choice towards a choice based on perceived educational quality"[58] has not, for fundamental, political reasons, led to any change in the system of equal support for public and private schools. This means that Dutch parents are more likely than those in most other countries to have a real choice between several schools in their community. So the social and educational outcomes of the Dutch system are of considerable interest to other countries.

Main characteristics

The equal subsidy to all Dutch schools, public or private, is very different from a "voucher" system proposed or operating in some countries. Rather than giving a grant to schools in direct proportion to the number of pupils enrolled, the Dutch government pays directly for teachers, buildings and other school costs. Private schools may charge fees only for extra-curricular activities. All schools must follow the same government rules with respect to administration and curriculum. The most significant difference between private and public schools is that only the former may turn away prospective pupils under certain prescribed conditions.

The principle that everybody should have access to the type of school desired is embodied in the conditions under which the State will finance the establishment of a new school. It must be able to show that it can attract a minimum number of students; the number is lower if there is no other school of the same category (Protestant, Catholic or secular) in the municipality. Similar rules dictate when a school must close. These rules have made the Netherlands unusual as a heavily-urbanised society that nevertheless tolerates very small schools – a combination that makes choices more real than in many countries. A recent OECD review of the Netherlands noted that such a system is costly, but accepted that "the central value of freedom of choice" was an aspect of Dutch education beyond debate at the present time.[59] The costs pointed out by the OECD have been cautiously addressed in subsequent reforms which have increased in many cases the minimum permitted school size.[60]

In 1990, 69 per cent of pupils in the Netherlands attended private primary schools and 73 per cent private secondary schools. These proportions have changed rather little in recent years (see table), although since the 1950s the Catholic share in primary education and the public share in secondary education have fallen considerably, while private secular primary schools have started to become significant with the fashion of alternative teaching styles such as Montessori. The fall in Catholic enrolments was partly caused by a higher-than-average drop in family size for Catholics. About half of the Catholic school loss in primary education went to public schools, and half to non-religious private schools – a small but growing sector.

Public and private enrolment shares in the Netherlands

	1950	1960	1970	1980	1990
% of primary pupils in:					
Public schools	27	27	27	32	31
Private schools	73	73	73	68	69
of which:					
– Protestant	28	27	28	28	29
– Catholic	43	44	43	37	34
– neutral	2	2	2	3	6
% of secondary pupils in:					
Public schools	43	35	28	28	27
Private schools	57	65	72	72	73
of which:					
– Protestant	19	22	27	27	27
– Catholic	29	35	41	39	37
– neutral	9	7	4	6	9

Source: Dutch Bureau of Statistics.

The Dutch belief in the right to choose schools is reflected also in liberal rules for choice within the public sector. In general, parents are free to send their children to any school within the municipality, although in some larger cities the choice is limited to a smaller district. Moreover, there is a guarantee of entry into any public school; if it becomes overcrowded, further accommodation must be found. This does not always mean that popular schools get new buildings: where total school rolls within a municipality are not rising, they must use spare classrooms within less popular ones, not necessarily from the same sector (public or private). So choice between independently-governed schools coexists with a significant degree of State co-ordination.

A further important characteristic of school differentiation in the Netherlands is the large number of secondary school types. At the age of 12, children are allocated to one of four tracks. In ascending order of status, these are: lower vocational, lower general, upper general and university-bound. Schools may offer any one of these, or a combination. Parents are in theory free to choose any track, but it is very hard in practice for them to go against the recommendation of the primary school principal.

History and politics

The present Dutch system was set up to produce choice of school based on religious freedom. It was established by a settlement in 1917 between the secular liberal class that had been dominant in the 19th century and the Christian-Democrat parties that have held or shared power since the turn of the 20th century. This settlement has endured, despite declining Church membership, the weakening of the influence of other agents of religious socialisation (unions, journals, clubs, etc.) and the declining religious emphasis of many Protestant and Catholic schools. A secularist, common-school lobby argues against the logic of the Dutch public-private choice system on the grounds that its original rationale – to underpin religious freedom – is now bogus, because people select schools mainly on other grounds. Yet it is precisely the popularity of many religious schools for reasons other than religion (discussed below) that is one of the two main factors that keep any consideration of an end to equal funding off the political agenda. The other main factor is the link between Protestant and Catholic schools and the Christian-Democratic parties.

Nevertheless, two present trends may sow the seeds of a long-term transformation of the system. One is the *realpolitik* of schools' behaviour when faced with a declining overall pupil population (which fell nearly 20 per cent in primary schools between 1980 and 1990) and tightening conditions for school viability. This has caused religious schools to accept pupils more freely from all religions and from none; some Catholic schools in Rotterdam and the Hague now have a majority of Muslims enrolled, for example. It has also caused Christian schools of different denominations to merges even with municipal schools. Of schools merging in 1993, 16 per cent involved both public and private schools, 16 per cent schools of different denominations and 9 per cent Christian and secular private schools. This continuing dilution of schools' religious identity may one day threaten their survival as a separate sector.

The second current development is a proposal to devolve more responsibility for managing the whole system from central government to municipalities. This could involve, for example, a greater local government role in planning capital provision across all sectors. That would potentially cause a conflict of interest for municipalities as the governor of public schools as well as planner of public and private provision. So a parallel development might be the creation of foundations to run municipal schools with some autonomy from local government. Municipalities would like this change, which would give them a strategic role, allowing rationalisation of local provision and the weighting of resources according to social need. Religious schools fear it, as they feel it would undermine their independence and in particular their automatic access to resources regardless of any planning decisions. So by mid-1993 this proposal, while backed by the coalition government, faced considerable hostility among Christian-Democrats and had an uncertain future.

Choice patterns in practice (see Case Study 1 for detailed example)

Survey evidence supports a general perception in the Netherlands that religion is now just one of several factors determining school choice. When asked what kind of primary school they prefer for their children, for example, 39 per cent of Catholics, 39 per cent of reformed Protestants and 13 per cent of Calvinists do not express a preference for their own denomination; in non-religious families, 28 per cent do not express a preference for a secular school.[61] Thus, a substantial minority of the Dutch population is inclined to look for schools across the traditional "pillars". Even among those who express a preference, many are willing to cross these divides in certain circumstances.

Many of the other criteria for choosing schools relate to individual circumstance. As in most countries, proximity is an important factor. For secondary schools, however, geographical closeness is not always as critical as in some countries because of a particular Dutch factor. The bicycle provides safe and easy access to a wide range of schools in most Dutch cities, making transport considerations independent of bus routes, public subsidies, etc. A stronger factor influencing a local choice of school is often the school that one's friends or siblings are attending.

Two factors that appear to be of growing importance in making choices are the perceived academic quality and the social and racial composition of schools. It is important to emphasize that there is no systematic distinction in this respect between public and private schools: it is not assumed that one kind is better, except in relation to particular local circumstance. Perceptions of academic quality are heavily influenced at the secondary level by the range of academic streams offered by each school. (This is explained in the Haarlem example in Case Study 1). The four different ability-related "tracks" in Dutch secondary education make meritocratic distinctions a fact of life in relation to school attendance. Social distinctions are perhaps newer, but in large cities with growing ethnic minority populations, there have been signs of "white flight" from schools with mainly Turks, Moroccans and other foreign-origin pupils. (Although an important part of this "white flight" – some 60 per cent – can be explained by the class composition of schools.) This has prompted fledgeling moves towards bussing (in Gouda) and magnet schools (in Amsterdam). An important aspect of class- or race-based clustering in the Netherlands is that it is in large part related to self-selection for particular schools rather than formal or practical barriers to enrolment. So genuine choice of school is not incompatible with *de facto* segregation.

Examples of impact

In seeking to explain the persistence and continued popularity of religious schools in an "irreligious society", Dronkers[62] distinguishes a number of key factors. Perhaps the most important is that religious schools appear to perform better than public ones in places, such as Amsterdam, where public schools are the norm, but that public schools perform better in regions where Catholic schools are "normal". Dronkers suggests that people who have taken a deliberate choice against the "norm" are more likely to create an "educational community in which pupils will perform better". Thus, the existence of pluralistic choice may be good not only for social well-being but also for pupil performance.

Dronkers also suggests that religious schools are attractive because of their "mild educational conservatism". This generalisation may not always hold, but there is no doubt that, for better or for worse, the Dutch system militates against certain kinds of "progressive" school reform – especially where professional opinion differs from parental preferences. This has been particularly apparent in attempts to reform lower secondary education. Central government has wanted to make it more "comprehensive", by bringing together the various ability-related tracks into single schools, by creating and extending the "bridge" year in which ability groups are initially supposed to be mixed together, and by having a greater common curriculum, even when students are divided by ability. These moves have made halting progress, partly because of the need to negotiate them with the various church organisations at national level, but also because parent pressures often push in other directions. This is illustrated in the case of the Haarlem schools described below, in terms of their response to market pressures to keep children of different abilities as separate as possible.

Conclusion: choice in the Dutch setting

A particular set of historical/political influences has created the Dutch system of equal funding of public and private schools, and is expected to sustain it for the foreseeable future. Yet, the implicit decision to retain this system, despite a substantial weakening of the socio-religious groupings that gave rise to it, may be attributed not just to historical precedent and party politics, but also to a valuing of pluralism.

The Dutch feel comfortable with the existence of difference in various ways. Their tradition of tolerance permits schools following different philosophies to co exist within a publicly-funded system. But the social conservatism of the Netherlands also makes the Dutch more comfortable with certain other differences that might be unacceptable elsewhere – systematic separation of secondary school children by ability, and *de facto* segregation in some cases by race and by class. Perhaps social/racial separation is acceptable partly because it has not become intense or universal. But it also worries the Dutch less than the Americans because it is not associated with profound *educational* difference. "Black" schools here are not always seen as "sink" schools. The idea of equal access to resources is matched by the concept of equal provision of a good standard of schooling. Underwritten by such guarantees, school choice is seen by most Dutch people as a positive influence in society.

New Zealand
Choice through school autonomy

Introduction

New Zealand's school system has moved rapidly from central control to wide-ranging autonomy for schools, governed by parent-elected boards and competing for pupils. These changes have potentially opened up choices, on the one hand for individual parents and pupils in terms of selecting schools, and on the other hand for parent-composed boards and communities more generally in terms of influencing the development of schools at a local level. But in each of these cases, the promise of choice is in danger of not being fulfilled. Parents' choices can be frustrated by the polarisation of schools into the popular and unpopular, followed by the careful selection of pupils by the schools in greatest demand. Communities' cohesion can be threatened by bitter competition between schools that can result from devolution to the school level.

New Zealand's school choice policies go further than most countries' but also have their own particularities and limitations. Perhaps the most radical aspect in international terms is the independence given to the school boards in terms of identifying and, where necessary, selecting their client markets. A significant limit is that the teachers' trade unions have prevented their pay from being controlled by schools under "bulk funding", except for a limited number of schools on an experimental basis. Another limitation is that popular schools, which have quickly become full, have not had resources to expand supplied from the centre.

As well as devolving power to schools and introducing open enrolment, the government has also tried to improve the types of school available. This has not always worked – for example nobody had, by 1993, applied to make a State school into a "designated character school" as provided by 1989 legislation. A provision with more enthusiastic take-up has been the funding of *Kura Kaupapa Maori*, schools aiming to maintain and preserve the Maori language. Furthermore, the government gives some financial support to private schools. Since 1975 there has also been provision for private schools to integrate into the public system while retaining their special (usually religious) character.

Main characteristics

Devolution to schools

Since 1989, each of New Zealand's 2 700 schools has been governed by boards of between five and seven trustees elected by parents, plus the head teacher, a staff representative and co-opted members. Each board is a legal body accountable to the local community and to the Minister of Education through a school charter. Their duties include appointing staff, taking responsibility for the non-teaching budget and applying to establish an enrolment scheme when the school is full.

Under "bulk funding", responsibility for budgets is devolved to schools on a formula based largely on pupil numbers, but also including elements for "equity" (a social weighting) and/or Maori language teaching. The big budget item that has been excluded from bulk funding, except to 71 schools on an experimental basis from 1992 to 1994, is teachers' pay. In opposing the extension of this experiment, teacher unions with broad support have argued that it could cause a shift of resources away from teaching and that it offers government an opportunity to give to trustees the "dirty work" of cutting staff.

Enrolment rules

All centrally-set zoning rules determining where a child may go to school have been abolished. All schools must accept all pupils, until they are in danger of becoming overcrowded. Then, they must apply to government for permission to set a limit on the numbers entering the school, and draw up an "enrolment scheme" determining whom should be admitted. There are no rules, other than basic human rights legislation, constraining the terms of these enrolment schemes. (For an illustration of these terms, see "Examples of impact" below).

Transport

Until 1994, State assistance for transport created a bias towards choosing one's nearest school. Free transport or reimbursement of transport costs was available only to the nearest State school or to a private or "integrated" school that was closer than the nearest State school. From 1994, however, schools are allowed to opt for "bulk funding" for transport assistance and distribute it how they wish, and for those who do not, parents will be entitled to a grant equal to the cost of transport to the nearest school even if they go further afield.

Educational Development Initiatives (EDIs)

Central government retains responsibility for allocating capital resources to schools, for structuring school provision and for determining which age groups each school may serve. In order to make the restructuring of schools in a local area more sensitive to local needs, Educational Development Initiatives have been established in some areas, as a means of local consultation over planning. Two illustrations of how these initiatives work are described in Case Study 16. Their biggest advantage has been to start to repair damaging divisions within communities that have sometimes resulted from competition between schools. Their drawbacks seem to be the cumbersome pace at which such consultation feeds through into specific proposals, and uncertainty over whether such proposals will be approved at the political level by central government.

Kura Kaupapa Maori

Since 1989, the government has agreed to provide funding to approved Maori-language schools, known as *Kura Kaupapa Maori*. About 25 such schools were in operation by the end of 1993; their development is discussed further in Case Study 10. Increasing support for Maori culture has been the government's most significant step in allowing choices for educational pluralism. In 1992, nearly 9 000 pupils had more than 50 per cent of their education taught in Maori in mainstream schools. However, there have also been objections that the Maori-language element in bulk funding for schools' operational grants is not always devoted to this purpose.

Independent schools

The New Zealand government has given varying levels of support for private schools, since 1976, in the form of teacher salary grants, ranging from 50 per cent between 1976 and 1985 to nothing from 1990 to 1991. Subsequently, a grant of 17 per cent rising to 20 per cent in 1993 was restored by the National (Conservative) government, with an expressed intention to raise it progressively to 50 per cent when circumstances permit. More important than the level of grant has been a change in rationale for the subsidy – not just to preserve the choice represented by the existence of these particular schools, but to support the continuation of private options for their own sake. Private schools enrol some 4 per cent of New Zealand schoolchildren.

Integrated schools

Since 1975, private schools have been able to "integrate" into the State system, while retaining aspects of their distinctive identity. This option has been taken mainly by Catholic schools. Most other independent schools saw disadvantages with the constraints put on them by integration, for example the need to increase pupil/teacher ratios. Since the Catholic schools had been badly resourced, they did not face this problem. Despite allowing these schools into the State system, the government protected existing public schools from competition for pupils from this sector, in a period of falling school rolls, by fixing a maximum roll number and limiting to 5 per cent the proportion of their pupils who could come from non-Catholic backgrounds. Ironically, in the more recent atmosphere of popular schools having to find ways of restricting numbers and selecting pupils, this has made things easier for many integrated schools.

History and politics

Before the late 1980s, New Zealand offered very little scope for choice of school within the public sector, and schools were governed largely by the central government, which exercised tight bureaucratic control. This system was changed rapidly and decisively at the initiative of a Labour government between 1987 and 1990, as part of a general policy of rethinking the way in which public services were delivered. An initial task force chaired by a prominent businessman, Brian Picot, in 1987/88 identified centralisation, bureaucracy and lack of accountability as severe weaknesses of the education system, and recommended devolution, dezoning and bulk funding. After a very short consultation period – six weeks including two weeks in school holidays – the government's plans were published in the document *Tomorrow's Schools,* which was then implemented.

The National government elected in November 1990 brought a new perspective to the reform process, relaxing the rules under which enrolment schemes could be established, improving support for private schools and looking for greater economies in the private sector. But in New Zealand, in a way quite similar to Sweden, the main thrust of school choice and of devolution has spanned the party divide. In New Zealand, the fiercest opposition and bitterness at what has been seen as damaging reforms based on "imported" ideologies have come from teacher unions and individual teachers. The principals' associations, on the other hand, have been broadly in favour, and secondary school principals in particular have welcomed the extra flexibility it has brought them.

Choice patterns in practice

The free choice of schools in New Zealand is too new for firm evidence to be available about how parents use it. However, widely held perceptions and provisional findings from the monitoring of the system point to:

- a continuing strong preference for the closest school, especially in rural areas and small towns;
- the emergence in larger cities, especially Auckland, of a perceived hierarchy of schools, with those at the top of the hierarchy tending to be in better-off districts;
- an intensification of this polarising trend by the setting-up of "enrolment schemes" to select pupils by schools threatened with overcrowding; these schools are seen as all the more desirable because they can be selective, by geographical or other criteria (see following section);
- perception of academic excellence being the most important choice criterion after location;[63]
- a widespread perception of private schools as being better, and public support for a policy of subsidising private schools (according to a recent opinion poll).[64]

Examples of impact

Choice, autonomy and competition immediately made New Zealand schools intensely concerned about their image; widespread advertising has become the norm. Other generalisations about changes in school behaviour will take longer to discern. But specific pieces of evidence are starting to emerge:

- The terms of enrolment schemes drawn up by schools threatened with overcrowding show some potentially worrying trends. Although area of residence is the most common criterion for allocating places, the shape of the priority enrolment area is not always symmetrical – and can potentially be used to restrict intake to more privileged neighbourhoods. Moreover, the arbitrariness in determining who goes to which popular school is often increased by the listing of "factors which will be taken into account, without any implied ranking" – which consequently allow the principal wide discretion about whom to admit, with no basis for appeal. In the case of one old-established boys' high school, these non-ordered criteria consist of:

"1. Residence of the student ... within the ... District.
2. Residents of the applicant beyond the ... District may give entitlement to enrolment on the basis of need or merit established by the headmaster.
3. The wish of the applicant to study a specialist subject or group of subjects perhaps not otherwise available.
4. Family connections with the school: brothers, sons and grandsons of Old Boys and sons of staff currently employed at the school.
5. The demonstrated character, motivation, performance and work habits of the applicant."

The lack of regulation of such criteria makes it possible for popular schools to define their clientele as they please, provided they do not infringe basic human rights legislation.
– The frustration of the wishes of some parents in being excluded from popular schools is inevitable given the inability of such schools to expand to meet demand. Capital resources are still tightly controlled by the government, but a review was being undertaken in 1993 to consider whether it should be devolved more to schools.
– The atomising of decision-making has caused much dissatisfaction in a country of tightly-knit, small communities with small schools. There is considerable insecurity about schools losing even a few pupils to neighbouring districts when that could threaten them with closure. Critics of this aspect of "choice" point out that the choices of a few can thus take away the choices of the many. Moreover, the fierce competition between schools within small towns has caused rifts seen as socially damaging. Educational Development Initiatives have attempted to heal that damage.

Conclusion: choice in the New Zealand setting

Critics of the education policies introduced in New Zealand at the end of the 1980s claimed that the government was introducing a "foreign ideology". It is true that the *Tomorrow's Schools* proposals were based to a large degree on perceptions of what was being done in the United Kingdom and elsewhere. But the attempt to create self-determination for schools genuinely played to one of New Zealand's strengths: the eagerness of local communities to control their own destiny. The risk is that such reforms could also threaten the consensus of local communities by setting one school against another.

Unlike in the United Kingdom and the United States, the choice idea has not been stimulated by a sense of widespread failure in New Zealand's public school system. The association between choice and the creation of a hierarchy of schools by quality is thus a potential threat to a system widely perceived to deliver acceptable standards of education across the board. The biggest political stimulus for reform was in fact fiscal – the idea that a locally-based school system could be run more economically. It is therefore not surprising that measures such as the Educational Development Initiatives are seen by many as a government cost-cutting exercise. For local decision-making and choice to win general support in New Zealand, communities will have to be shown more clearly how such changes can be of net benefit to their interests.

Sweden
A dose of competition in a decentralising system

Introduction

Sweden's school system has had an international reputation for both quality and equality, but a local reputation for also being monochrome and unresponsive. Reforms initiated by a Social-Democrat government and extended by a Conservative one have attempted to decentralise decision-making and open up the system to greater parental influence.

The key change made by the Social-Democrats was the devolution of school funding and management in 1991, from a national board to municipalities. The key change made by the Conservatives was a law passed in 1992 requiring municipalities to give a grant to each private school based on 85 per cent of the cost of educating a pupil in the local public system. Enrolment rules have also been opened up in the public sector, with money following pupils – although to a varying extent, in practice, in different municipalities.

These changes, while new, appear to have increased competition among Swedish schools and opened up new choices at the margin. Choice has not become an active process for most Swedish parents, in that there is still a strong inclination to attend one's assigned local public school. Private school attendance is extremely low by international standards. Nevertheless, the "power of exit" has become a potential weapon for parents, especially in urban areas. Many schools have become more responsive to parents' wishes, and some have tried to build a more distinctive identity. The challenge for the Swedish system will be to retain a high-quality and coherent school system, while using parental involvement and the pressure for distinctiveness towards constructive educational purposes.

Main characteristics

Public support for private schools

Since 1992, municipalities have been required to give a recurrent grant to any independent school providing ordinary compulsory schooling which has been approved by the National Agency for Education. Legislation requires a school to be approved:

"if the education of the school provides knowledge and skills, the nature and level of which essentially correspond to the knowledge and skills conveyed by compulsory schooling and if in other essential respects the school conforms to the general goals of compulsory schooling."[65]

The grant is for at least 85 per cent of the cost of educating a pupil in the local municipal system, multiplied by the number of pupils in the school.

This provision has led to an increase in the number of private schools, but they remain small both in terms of their average size and in terms of the percentage of Swedish schoolchildren enrolled in them. During the first full year of the subsidy system, 1992/93, 9 946 pupils were enrolled. This was a rise of 20 per cent in private enrolments, but represented only 1.1 per cent of all pupils. However, these schools were concentrated in densely-populated areas, and 3.5 per cent of compulsory-age pupils attended private schools in cities larger than 200 000. Private schools enrolled on average 94 pupils.

Fees at Swedish private schools have always (with a few exceptions) been modest; typically, SKr 5 000 a year. The new subsidy system appears to be reducing dependence on fees, with nearly 90 per cent of the schools approved during the 1992/93 school year charging no fees at all. Of those approved previously, half were not charging fees in mid-1993.

Choice within the public sector

Swedes have traditionally had little or no possibility of attending a public compulsory school other than the local one to which they are assigned. This lack of choice has reflected the assumption that all schools are more or less equal, and provide a uniform basic education. The very term *Grundskola*, or "basic school", for the nine compulsory years (ages 7-16) is significant.

Preliminary attempts to improve choice within the public sector have affected both the demand side, in terms of parents'/pupils' ability to choose, and the supply side, in terms of enabling schools to become different. As yet, progress on both sides has been modest in comparison to the situation in many other countries, but significant in the Swedish context.

The right of parents to apply for schools outside their catchment area was first introduced in qualified form by the Social-Democrats in 1991, and consolidated by bills passed by the Conservatives in 1992 and in 1993. However, the entitlement to choose one's school is tempered by:

- *The fact that almost all municipalities continue to allocate a school to each child on the basis of residence, with an active choice needed only in order to go elsewhere.* Thus, "choice" in the Swedish public sector is officially presented as a rejection of a presumed option rather than a selection among alternatives.
- *The priority universally given to children within the catchment area when a school is full.* This limits the scope for active choice of popular schools regardless of residence.
- *The varying degree to which money for public schools follows pupils' choices.* Some municipalities, notably Stockholm and Helsingborg (see Case Studies 4 and 8), linked substantial proportions of school funding to student numbers in the early 1990s. In Stockholm it is estimated that 50 per cent of money for schools follows student enrolment decisions – not exceptionally high by international

standards, but enough to give a strong incentive to schools to enrol and retain pupils. Many other municipalities have not gone nearly as far.

On the supply side, schools in many municipalities have been encouraged to specialise more, by taking on "profiles" in terms of being strong in certain areas such as music or technology (see Case Study 8 for an example). However, these differences have not had a major impact on educational content and to a large extent serve to reinforce a school's identity. A more significant attempt to encourage differences between schools has come with legislation reforming the compulsory school curriculum, which reduces prescription of how much time should be spent teaching particular subjects, although it specifies broad goals and assesses achievement more rigorously.

Reforms to the upper secondary curriculum are also likely to have a significant effect on choice. There has always been considerable choice within upper secondary schools, in terms of many alternative vocational or general academic subject lines that may be studied. This has led to the fear that specific vocational courses follow student demand, regardless of the number of jobs available in each occupational area, with resulting mismatches between skills and available jobs. The new curriculum replaces 500 specific occupational and academic lines with 16 national programmes representing broad subject areas, on the basis that flexible rather than occupation-specific skills are needed in today's workforce. While this reduces choice of programme, it increases choice within programmes, allowing students to take greater responsibility for the structure of their studies.

Devolution of financial responsibilities

The devolution of financial responsibility for schools from a National Board of Education (abolished in 1991) to local municipalities was a radical change to the Swedish system. It is not in the scope of this study to report on devolution as such. But one of the intentions of devolution was to create a greater awareness of educational costs at a local level, together with greater flexibility over spending, and hence to devolve key choices. To some extent, in the context of fiscal crisis, this can be seen as devolution of responsibility for cost-cutting. But it is also evident that decentralisation has created a greater awareness of and dialogue about the choices available, among local government, schools and parents, who had previously regarded education policy as something handed down from the centre.

A starting point has been the need for municipalities to calculate something they previously had no idea of: the average cost of educating a student. This calculation is necessary in order to determine the subsidy to private schools, but has also encouraged municipalities to reassess the basis on which they allocate money to public ones. Trends in Sweden and elsewhere indicate that devolution of responsibility will continue from municipalities to schools, with parents' choices increasingly determining the allocation of resources.

History and politics

Until the middle of the 19th century, most Swedish children were educated either at home or in an extensive network of private schools. The present nine-year compulsory school was not introduced until 1962, but the decision to create a universal, public and egalitarian school system was quickly carried through to an extreme. By the early 1980s, only 0.6 per cent of children were attending private schools, and even these schools were regulated. Unlike in many countries, home schooling is not a legal option in Sweden.

Questioning of this monochrome system began with the appointment by a Conservative government in 1979 of an "Independent Schools Committee" to look into private schooling. For much of the 1980s, governments discussed tentatively whether there was a need for more private schools to enrich educational innovation. This led eventually to the bill passed by the Conservatives in 1992, allowing money to follow pupils to the private sector. This took more of a demand-led perspective than some of the earlier discussions about private providers creating a more diversified supply: choice, said the bill, "can stimulate greater involvement in education on the part of parents, and wider response to the preferences of pupils and parents on the part of schools and municipal authorities".[66]

In the late 1980s the Social-Democrats also started to discuss whether the public sector itself could be liberalised to accommodate a wider variety of civic demands. Legislation increasing somewhat the room for curriculum specialisation was intended to give schools the ability to create "profiles" that would enable parents to choose between them. The Conservatives, while continuing to allow more flexibility within the curriculum, have again stressed the demand side in relation to choice between public schools, with legislation guaranteeing more clearly the right to enrol anywhere.

Thus, while there are political differences over the degree of subsidy for private schools and the degree of openness of public sector enrolment, there has been a broad consensus to move in these directions. But while the Social-Democrats, still planners by instinct, tend to focus on managed diversity, the Conservatives stress the idea of putting power into the hands of the consumer. Their particular aim is to strengthen the power of exit, with the object of forcing schools to listen to and involve parents, rather than necessarily creating a spectrum of different schools to choose from.

Choice patterns in practice

Since school choice in Sweden has been severely constrained until very recently, research into how Swedes choose schools is sparse. But a survey of parents carried out in 1993 for the National Agency for Education[67] provides interesting preliminary evidence. Among its findings:
- 7 per cent of parents had ever chosen a school other than the assigned public one, of whom three-quarters had had this choice fulfilled.
- Of those who had not previously chosen, 17 per cent had considered doing so, but only 6 per cent thought they would choose in the next year.
- 59 per cent of parents think that if they are allowed to choose schools, teachers will work harder.
- 75 per cent of parents had heard of the school reforms; 47 per cent felt they were informed about the options available.
- Parents who have selected schools outside their catchment area have tended to cite a wide range of reasons. Teaching quality and atmosphere were cited almost universally – by 97 per cent of respondents.

– Choice among schools is only a reality in the larger cities; in many rural areas the main interest is in the choice of having a local school rather than not having one.

Overall, the picture seems to be one of growing awareness of school choice, but with the great majority of parents continuing to send their children to the allocated neighbourhood school.

Examples of impact

It is too early to draw any sweeping conclusions about the impact of choice on school behaviour, on the long-term development of private schooling or on social segregation between schools. However, the following points should be noted:
– *Choice has put new pressures on public schools, which previously had had a completely "captive" market.* In particular, schools for the first time have actively started to "market" themselves to parents, for example by producing brochures and other information. The tendency to announce "profiles" for schools, noted above, has so far been seen to a large degree as part of an image-making strategy rather than in terms of changing significantly a school's educational offerings.
– *Most private schools are in one of three categories.* Before the general subsidy was introduced, the majority had either a pedagogical (Montessori or Waldorf) or religious philosophy. Both these categories have grown, most notably schools of an Evangelical Christian character. But a third category, less well represented in the past but growing fast under the new policy, is "ordinary" schools, with no particular philosophy. These accounted for nearly half of schools approved in the 1992/93 school year. They often result from the desire of a community to open or retain a school when the municipality has decided otherwise. Since their grant is based on average pupil costs locally rather than nationally, such schools tend to get a higher than average subsidy. This direction of resources according to private decision-making, to purposes which public decision-making has declared uneconomical, is broadly approved by the government, which stresses the importance of conscious community backing for a school.
– *As in many countries, critics of choice warn that in the large cities it is increasing social segregation.* While it is hard to find general evidence of this, specific examples are already apparent, as illustrated in Case Study 4 below. Research indicates that Swedish education has never been completely socially-neutral as sometimes supposed, and that social differentiation has continued in terms of both school attendance and school results.[58] Potentially, a weakening of the link between school attendance and residence could reduce social segregation, but many commentators believe that it is more likely to increase it.

Conclusion: choice in the Swedish setting

To allow parents a free choice of public or State-subsidised private school was a radical move for Sweden, where choice had previously been so limited. But limits to the impact that this is likely to have on the school system are dictated in large part by the attitude of consumers. Swedes have on the whole been happy with the quality of their schools, but have often complained about their lack of influence. Giving them the power of choice has not broken the pattern of most selecting the local municipal school, but has started to change their relationship with that school. More parents than in the past feel that they are listened to.

Choice might well end up creating greater social and racial segregation among schools, at the margins, in some of Sweden's larger cities. This has not yet led to widespread alarm, partly because social consensus is higher and the class divide less intense than in many countries. An important aspect of this is that most Swedes perceive schools as being of equal educational quality. Variations in school results are attributed in the public mind to differences in social intake, but there is not the sense that going to a "middle-class" school will automatically give any one child an educational advantage.

The United States
In search of an acceptable choice

Introduction

School choice has been hotly debated in the United States, but unevenly pursued. The local nature of educational responsibilities has prevented any national policy changes like in the United Kingdom, Sweden and New Zealand. The most controversial aspect of the national debate has been over whether to allow public money to pay for private schooling. But various "choice" policies that have been implemented at the state and local levels have related primarily to choice within the public sector.

The intensity of the American choice debate has been caused by a conjunction of two factors. On the one hand, general opportunities to choose have been limited by the compartmentalisation of public school zones and districts and by the lack of any subsidy to private schools. On the other hand, better-off families have increasingly been choosing in practice to escape public schools with bad reputations, either by moving to districts with better schools or by buying private education. Advocates of public vouchers for private education say they wish to give poorer families the same opportunities as richer ones. Opponents claim that support for private schools would mean further support for the privileged and further deterioration of public schools. By 1993, only one, very limited, voucher scheme was in operation – in Milwaukee, Wisconsin.

Policies to improve choice within the public sector, on the other hand, have been introduced in a large number of states. The right to select a school across a district boundary and to choose among schools within one's home district have been extended. More radically, a few choice plans require every parent within a district to make an active choice of school, and give no priority according to place of residence. The United States also has considerable experience of schools with special characteristics, linked to choice, starting in the 1970s with "magnet" school programmes with racial desegregation as the main objective.

Main characteristics

Although the states are constitutionally responsible for education, provision is almost everywhere left to more local school districts with elected governing boards. There are 15 000 of these districts, and conditions under which a choice of school may be exercised vary considerably. But the following characteristics are significant to the context of recent choice initiatives:

- Choice of public school has until recently been restricted mainly to one's district of residence, even though many school districts are extremely small. A number of districts have only one elementary, junior high or high school.
- School districts within a state often devote widely different levels of resources to schooling.
- Within most districts with a number of schools, pupils are assigned to elementary (ages 6-12) and junior high (ages 12-15) schools according to residential zones. However, principals may often accept transfers when space is available, and are encouraged to do so when this will reduce racial segregation.
- In the case of high schools (ages 15-18), choices are often available within districts. The "comprehensive high school" idea is tempered by differences in programmatic orientation which for many years linked some high schools to certain client groups (for example "classical", "technical" or "vocational" labels). The emergence of "alternative" schools and "magnet" schools (see below) further increased this diversity.
- Over five million American schoolchildren (11 per cent of the total) attend private schools – a high proportion, considering that these schools get no direct public support. (But tax dollars are spent on two important services for children at private schools: school bussing and "Chapter 1" funds, to help educationally disadvantaged students.) About half of private school enrolments are at Catholic schools and 84 per cent are at schools with some religious identity. A minority of private schools are high-prestige and expensive; the great mass are associated with and subsidised by local churches; a third category is those established recently by alternative religious, ethnic or philosophical movements, but many of these lead an uncertain existence with scant resources.

The following types of initiative linked with school choice are of particular interest:

Inter-district choice

In 1987, Minnesota became the first state to oblige all its districts to accept transfers across district boundaries (see Case Study 13). In the following three years, seven other states followed its example. In addition, desegregation programmes permitting transfers between urban and suburban districts in large metropolitan areas have been introduced around Boston, Kansas City, Milwaukee and other cities.

More choice within districts

It is impossible to classify all the different ways in which new kinds of school have been introduced into American school districts. The two most common classifications, which to some extent overlap, are "alternative" and "magnet" schools. Alternative schools for potential drop-outs or pupils with special talents emerged from the 1960s onwards, as a response to interest in informal, pupil-centred schooling. Magnet schools, with a particular theme or programme, were established widely from the 1970s onwards, usually to satisfy court-ordered desegregation without having to force children to go to geographically-remote schools. The "magnet" effect of the programme aimed to secure desegregation by choice rather than compulsion, although this often means excluding many local pupils of the over-represented race in a popular school whose numbers need to be balanced. In some districts, a large proportion of schools, or even all of them, have acquired magnet status (see Case Study 9). "It seems reasonable to generalise", writes Charles Glenn in his background report to this study, "that some measure of variety among public schools is provided in most school systems operating a dozen or more schools."[69]

New ways of choosing within districts

The following variations on allocation to school by zone have been introduced in certain districts:
- *open enrolment,* under which pupils can transfer to any school on a space-available basis;
- *controlled transfer,* under which transfer is permitted only where it improves racial balance;
- *enrolment in magnet schools* which give equal priority, subject to racial balance, to all pupils in the district;
- *enrolment in magnet programmes* housed in schools that otherwise draw their enrolment from a residential attendance zone;
- *"universal" choice,* under which school attendance districts are abolished and all pupils are assigned to schools according to stated preferences, with little or no priority by residence. Although rare, this system has spread to 16 cities in Massachusetts.[70]

Challenges to the school district monopoly

The well-publicised critique of bureaucratic control of schools by Chubb and Moe[71] in 1990 is unlikely to lead to the creation of self-governing schools, as its authors advocate. But for the first time, models of managing public schools other than by school districts are emerging, notably:
- *"Charter" schools, governed independently of school districts and funded directly by the state.* Several states have enacted legislation allowing a limited number of charter schools under carefully controlled conditions. In Minnesota (see Case Study 13), these conditions include approval by the district authorities; in California there are fewer restrictions but, as in Minnesota, a limit on the number of schools. A key characteristic of charter schools is exemption from many regulations.
- *The contracting of the management of schools by the school district.* "Educational Alternatives Inc.", a Minnesota-based private company, has been contracted to run some schools in Miami and Baltimore. The Edison Project, also set up by a private company, aims to develop an improved model of schooling. Although the main aim is to run private schools, it is intended that the per-pupil cost will be no greater than in public education, and the project may also create and run public schools if invited by districts. The non-profit-making sector is getting involved too: in 1988, Boston University signed a contract with the school board in Chelsea, Massachusetts, to run all of its schools for ten years.

Public support for private schools

There has been much debate over "vouchers" for private education, but only two examples of implementation, both limited:
- In Alum Rock, California, during the 1970s, "vouchers" were introduced which pupils were allowed to take to any school, public or private. Although frequently cited as America's first experiment with vouchers, this experience was highly limited, not least by the fact that no private school actually participated. It eventually turned into a public sector open-enrolment programme.
- In Milwaukee, Wisconsin, poor pupils have been given vouchers to attend private schools since 1990. This experiment, described in Case Study 15, is limited to non-religious schools and to 1 per cent of children in the city's public school system. Despite its limitations, it is being watched carefully by both advocates and opponents of vouchers in the United States.

History and politics

School choice has been a theoretical issue in the United States at least since Milton Friedman first made the case for school vouchers in 1962.[72] But the first and perhaps most significant steps that improved school choice were not motivated, as Friedman was, by competition but by a desire for social justice. Alternative programmes for disadvantaged groups, and magnet schools as a voluntary means of achieving desegregation where compulsory school bussing had failed, drew support in the 1960s and 1970s from campaigners for the disadvantaged. This element of school choice remains important in the United States, and is in the 1990s personified in Milwaukee's Polly Williams, the charismatic black exponent of using school vouchers to give opportunities to poor children whom public schools have failed.

Another important strand affecting the American choice debate has been a halving of enrolments in Catholic schools since the early 1960s, largely because many Catholics moved out of the inner cities where they were located, and fewer free services were provided by monks and nuns, making it harder to offer cheap private schooling to the lower- and middle-income groups. Research by Coleman and others appearing to show that private religious schools are more effective than public ones[73] made the debate more intense during the 1980s, with many arguing that today's poor, non-Catholic residents of inner cities could benefit if such schools were subsidised. Supporters of religious schools clashed with upholders of the secular tradition of public support for schooling, upheld by a constitutional ban on public aid to a religion. At the same time many liberal defenders of public education opposed what they saw as attempts to undermine it by those with a stake in the private system.

In the late 1980s, the debate moved centre-stage in educational politics, with the re-emergence of the competition argument, as the latest strand in attempts to reform America's public schools after the publication of *A Nation at Risk* in 1983.[74] Attempts to improve school quality through existing structures were perceived to be failing; choice and competition have been seen as a means of shaking up the system and subjecting it to new pressures. Chubb and Moe in 1990[75] argued that democratic control through district school boards created a stultifying layer of bureaucracy and negotiated decision-making that prevented schools from finding dynamic solutions to educational problems.

In the 1990s, this mix of pressures is provoking two broad types of response. One is a concerted effort by a coalition of interests to get legislation for vouchers for private school tuition. In 1992, those efforts either failed to get on state ballots or were voted down, but a renewed attempt was being made in California in 1993. In their favour, advocates can point to a high and apparently growing proportion of the public who express support for the principle of vouchers.[76] Their biggest political difficulty is the fact that vouchers would increase taxes, by paying for the education of the 11 per cent of Americans who at present pay for it themselves. It has been easy to exploit that at the polls in tax-averse America.

Some observers saw the defeat of President George Bush, who publicly supported "private school choice" as signifying a shift of emphasis to choice within the public sector. These efforts attract a politically more diverse coalition of support, including former civil rights reformers who see choice as opening up avenues for the underprivileged, and some educationalists who wish to try out new ideas.

Choice patterns in practice

It is impossible to generalise about how Americans choose schools in practice, as there is no single policy determining how they can choose. Moreover, much research has focused on parents' *attitudes* towards choice in an attempt to prove or disprove the case for vouchers or other reforms. The popularity of many magnet schools shows that programme emphasis can be a significant reason for choosing, a finding supported by various studies.[77]

But what is perhaps most distinctive about choice of schools in the United States is how often it is linked to choice of residence. Americans move house often, and frequently consider school quality as an essential of neighbourhood character. This makes choice of school for social reasons impossible to distinguish fully from choice for educational reasons. A 1984 study in Minnesota found that 62 per cent of public school parents considered themselves "active" choosers, compared to 53 per cent of private school parents. But only 26 per cent of public school parents had considered other schools at the time they chose their present one, compared to 34 per cent of private school parents. Rather, most had considered public school quality when deciding where to live.[78]

Examples of impact

As with so many innovations in the United States, it is impossible to generalise about the impact of innovations with such varied characteristics as school choice policies. Four examples are included in the case studies below. It is also worth noting here that:
– *Studies on educational impact tend to show that certain kinds of school (private schools, alternative schools) appear to have superior results, discounting for pupil background.*[79] But they do not prove that choice itself, rather than the schools' defining characteristics, produces these results.

- *Magnet schools appear to have an extremely varied impact that depends to a large degree on the design of the programme.* Research in Chicago and other large cities[80] reveals that they can become a "new improved sorting machine", increasing social class segregation. Other studies[81] conclude that well-designed magnet systems have improved racial and social integration more effectively than forced bussing.
- *Inter-district choice of public schools has effects that vary according to circumstance and the nature of the policy.* The financial relationships between districts is crucial. In Massachusetts, for example, some rich districts spend twice as much per elementary school child as some poor ones. When a child takes the attractive option of travelling to school in a better-resourced town, the home district must transfer this higher cost to the receiving district, leaving it both worse off and with less viable schools. So polarisation in opportunities in different places intensifies. In Minnesota on the other hand, inter-district differences are lower, there is more state equalisation of resources, and transfers from sending to receiving districts are based on the state-wide average cost of educating a child.

Conclusion: choice in the American setting

The debate over school choice epitomises the competing American values of individual freedom, individual opportunity and social justice. American parents are far more inclined than, for example, Swedish ones to see schooling as a route to social mobility and economic success for their children. They are therefore inclined to take advantage of opportunities to choose schools according to their relative quality – the more so in times when standards in some public schools are widely regarded as unsatisfactory. The big counterbalance to individualism in American education, the "common" public school, is breaking down as an institution, as middle-class flight from city districts in particular are making it a ghetto institution.

Nevertheless, there has been a greater hesitation than in Sweden or Australia to give public support to pupils who choose private schools, and less extensive measures for public sector choice than in New Zealand or the United Kingdom. One important reason is the fragmentation of decision-making, together with political structures that resist radical change. But in addition, the fear that choice might work against social justice has been more convincing in a country where more people seem inclined to behave as individualistic, choosy consumers than in Europe.

Yet, high awareness of the social consequences of choice has also meant that, unlike elsewhere, there have been explicit attempts in the United States to design choice policies that are socially just. Some magnet programmes, alternative schools and "universal" choice schemes, for example, have sought to counter the unequal educational opportunities available to people of different class, race or neighbourhood. The continuing, if uneven, efforts of Americans to introduce "responsible" choice programmes are therefore worth watching.

Part III
SIXTEEN CASE STUDIES

SIXTEEN CASE STUDIES

Case Study 1

Haarlem

School choice in a Dutch city

In this medium-sized city in the west of the Netherlands, some of the main features of choice in the Dutch education system can be illustrated. All four of the main Dutch school types – public, Catholic, Protestant and private-secular – are present. Full public funding for "private" schools means that price does not constrain choice (small fees are charged for extra-curricular activities only). Parents choose actively among the schools, religious character being just one of many criteria used to decide. More important in the majority of cases are geography, perceived educational quality and atmosphere. In the case of secondary schools, the way the school places itself in the four-track separation of students is possibly the most important criterion. Parents' aspirations for their children are, on average, rising as parents' own educational levels increase, and they tend to look for schools focusing on higher tracks. This can work against the central government's aim of encouraging comprehensive schools, and might also intensify social polarisation, in particular between Dutch origin and immigrant groups.

Characteristics

Haarlem has 150 000 inhabitants, most of them fairly affluent, but also including a significant minority of poorer immigrant groups, mainly from Turkey and Morocco. The number of school pupils declined by about 40 per cent between the late 1970s and early 1990s, when there were some 10 000 children enrolled in the city's 50 primary schools and 8 000 in 15 secondary.

About half of the schools are public, 40 per cent are Catholic or Protestant and 10 per cent private secular schools. Nine primary schools with particular methods (Montessori, etc.) are, atypically for the Netherlands, mainly in the *public* sector, as a result of decisions by politicians to offer a spectrum of choices. There has also been a conscious policy to create a large special school sector, and the 20 special schools attract pupils from a wide geographical area.

Two kinds of change that are being proposed more generally in the Netherlands are already, to a considerable extent, being implemented by Haarlem's municipal authorities. First, there has been considerable devolution of power to public schools, with principals getting more control over budgets and teacher recruitment. The municipality wants to be seen more as a service centre than as a manager of its schools. Second, and in parallel with its move away from a management role, the municipality attempts to some extent to act as a co-ordinator of school provision in the city – including in the private sector. There is, at least, somewhat more dialogue between public and private education in Haarlem than in some Dutch cities. One small but revealing example of this is the response to refugees arriving in the city from the former Yugoslavia after its break-up: the extra school places and social support needed for these groups were planned jointly by the authorities of municipal and private schools.

Choice patterns

Choosing a school in Haarlem is generally an active process. All schools have open days, in January or February, at which parents and children are able to visit the buildings and talk to staff and pupils. Typically, they look at two or three secondary schools before making a choice. Among the criteria for choosing are:
- *Religion, which for a minority of parents is the most important factor.* There is no firm evidence on the size of this minority, but most observers estimate it at around 20 per cent. The view that it is small is supported by two elements. First, the mixed religious affiliations of pupils in every kind of school in the city. For example, there are as many children from Catholic families in public schools as in Catholic ones. The second element, widely perceived in the city and criticised by some religious families, is the waning religious character of schools calling themselves Catholic and Protestant. This is partly linked to the increasingly mixed clientele: with falling overall school rolls and a decline in the numbers affiliated in particular to the Catholic Church, many schools know that they cannot survive unless they diversify.
- *Residence.* In the case of primary schools, many parents make a choice between just one or two possibilities in the local area. In the case of secondary schools, residence is less important, in the sense that parents and children consider schools over a much wider area – typically three or four. One factor that creates a different situation from, say, many American cities or suburbs is the bicycle as a means of student transport, combined with the superb network of bicycle lanes that make cycling safe. Pupils feel quite happy cycling half an hour or more to and from school, which gives a wide range of possibilities. However, students are often influenced, if not by distance, then by the choices of their primary school friends, so there are strong associations between particular primaries and particular secondaries. Moreover, at both levels schools display social profiles corresponding to the surrounding population – particularly in the south of the city, where secondary schools are fed by pupils from extremely affluent nearby villages. These residential characteristics are certainly more important influences on a school's social profile than whether it is public or "private".
- *School quality and atmosphere.* Pupils, parents, teachers, head-teachers and the municipal education authorities all perceive that choice is being influenced to an increasing extent by perceptions of schools' quality and culture. Traditionally, schools of the same level have been regarded as educationally equal, making religion and residence the main choice criteria. The education authorities have encouraged more active choosing, by requiring schools to hold open days – which

have been well attended. In choosing between secondary schools, parents are strongly influenced by their children's preferences. According to one parent, children tend to judge by the character and "feel" of the building; parents more by conversations with teachers and hearsay from other parents. More scientific judgements are made difficult by the cautious attitude towards the publishing of results. The municipality requires schools to produce annual reports but does not publish them. One strong argument against publishing pupil results by school in the Netherlands is the danger that private schools would then exploit one of their few significant differences with public ones: the right to refuse pupils. This could be used to keep out less able pupils who might damage the grade average.

– *Race.* The sharp *de facto* segregation that is emerging in schools in some large Dutch cities is not at a chronic level in Haarlem, in the sense that there is no severe "white flight" from a particular school by Dutch origin families living near it. However, there are some schools with 70-80 per cent ethnic minority pupils, mainly Turk and Moroccan. This is partly a matter of geographical concentration, but also heavily influenced by decisions taken by ethnic minority families. Perhaps the most worrying element of these decisions relates to the choice of secondary school type, as described under the next criterion. In many schools leading to university and higher vocational education, there are no more than a handful of ethnic minority pupils; there is a big concentration in the schools following the lowest vocational track. This appears in large part due to low parental aspirations, and an anxiety about children faring badly in an environment where they are isolated from their ethnic group. On the other hand, schools dominated by Dutch origin pupils do little to discourage these attitudes or to seek a more varied ethnic mix. The highly-polarised result is interesting because it derives entirely from choices rather than rules: there are no formal barriers excluding ethnic groups from higher-status schools.

– *Secondary school types.* Choice at the secondary school level depends to a large extent on the Dutch tracking system. Schools in the Netherlands offer one or more of the following tracks starting at age 13:
  • lower vocational ("VBO", to age 16);
  • lower general ("MAVO", to age 16; typically followed by upper secondary vocational schooling or apprenticeships);
  • higher general ("HAVO", to age 17; typically followed by higher vocational);
  • university-bound ("VWO", ending at 18, divided into *gymnasium*, which includes Greek and Latin, and *atheneum*, which does not).

Although many schools have traditionally followed just one of these tracks, there has been an increasing tendency to provide several in a single school, partly because falling rolls have made mergers necessary. The choice of track is mainly determined by the primary school's recommendation, based on the pupil's performance. But in choosing between schools that offer the assigned track, many parents are keen that their children should mix only with children from higher tracks than their own, rather than lower ones. They fear that in the "bridge class" (age 12-13) in which all children in a school in principle follow the same curriculum, mixing with lower-ability groups could harm their children's advantage. One significant factor in Haarlem is that the only pure *gymnasium* is in the public sector – this is the highest-status option, regardless of one's religion.

So parents and children actively choose their schools. Do schools also select pupils? There are conflicting claims about how far private schools exercise their right to keep out pupils whom they find undesirable, but this does not appear to be a major determining factor. More interesting in the international context is the guarantee in principle of a place in any public school to whoever applies. One constraint on choice in practice is the academic selectivity of schools at secondary level guided by primary school recommendations. If a pupil judged less able insists on a place, the school cannot refuse it, but might prevent the pupil from progressing to higher grades if he/she fails the end-of-year examinations. For schools with more eligible pupils than desks, there are two possibilities. One is to build to expand capacity, but funding will not be available unless the public school rolls in the municipality as a whole are rising. Alternatively, a school has the right to house classes at other school buildings where rolls have been falling, including, since 1979, in religious schools. One popular public school in Haarlem therefore runs some classes in a nearby Catholic school.

Three secondary schools

The following examples illustrate briefly how three kinds of secondary school in Haarlem place themselves in the educational "market":
- *Mendelcollege* is a Catholic school in North Haarlem with 750 pupils in the top two tracks (university-bound and higher general). In August 1993 this school was merging with two nearby, smaller schools, one Catholic and one Protestant, providing the next-lowest track (lower general). The decision was motivated by falling rolls, especially in the two smaller schools, which threatened their survival. But there is some fear in Mendelcollege that this change will make the university-bound and higher general options less attractive, because the character of the school will become "diluted". Until now, the school has attracted pupils over a wide area, with only 37 per cent of pupils coming from the two closest primary-school districts, and 37 per cent travelling from outside North Haarlem. Interestingly, the worry about diluting the *academic* character is not (except among a small minority) reflected with concerns about dilution of *religious* character caused by the merger with a Protestant school to become a hybrid "Christian school". The most important characteristic associated with being a Catholic school is not religious teaching but a "familial" rather than pure academic atmosphere. Most teachers are confident that this can be retained. Even as a Catholic school, a minority of 40 per cent of pupils are Catholic, about 40 per cent have no denomination and most of the rest are Protestant.
- *Eerste Christelijk Lyceum* is a Protestant school in south Haarlem with 630 pupils. Like Mendelcollege, it offers the higher general and university-bound tracks, but has no plans to widen this. On the contrary, concern that it is losing some bright Protestant pupils to the municipal *gymnasium* because their parents want a more rarefied intellectual environment caused the school to discontinue mixed-ability classes for 12-13 year-olds from academic year 1992/93. *This is a good example of an educational change prompted directly by parental choices.* Eerste Christelijk Lyceum is short of pupils: it could take 900. But the decision to try to win back high-ability pupils lost to the *gymnasium* rather than to broaden its base by merging was perhaps not the best option in purely financial terms. The school's strong, parent-dominated Association would not be happy to expand overall numbers if this meant fewer university-bound pupils. Indeed, the school

prides itself on being a small, academically-oriented institution. It is also proud of having a firm Christian character, a 70-year history and an old building to match.

– **Coornhert Lyceum** is a public school covering all levels of secondary education except lower vocational. Its 940 pupils are attracted to the school by a lively and relatively informal atmosphere, in which parents participate more actively than in many Dutch public schools. The head teacher considers the diversity of pupil abilities to be an advantage, both because she believes that younger children develop well in a mixed-ability environment, and because it allows children to change tracks without changing schools. However, pressure from some parents has influenced the setting-up of one optional high-ability class for 12-13 year-olds. Some children on the university-entrance track nevertheless choose the mixed-ability option at this level.

Despite making a virtue of its diversity and comprehensiveness, Coornhert Lyceum feels the need in an increasingly competitive environment to make itself distinctive. It has done this mainly by emphasizing its existing strength in music, and by developing a new special emphasis on mathematics and science.

Commentary

Schools in Haarlem can take students much less for granted than in the past. Competition is becoming more intense because of the combination of falling rolls and greater discernment by parents no longer so strongly bound by traditional religious ties. Although atmosphere and convenience are important factors, academic criteria are becoming increasingly significant in the choice of secondary schools, against the background of rising parental aspirations. This is partly a question of schools adapting to the falling demand for the lower educational tracks. But it also creates pressures for schools to emphasize the needs of the most able students, in responding to their parents' desire to create a separate education. This makes it hard for those educators who believe in the effectiveness of mixed-ability schooling to apply this principle in secondary schools. Moreover, as a growing number of Dutch origin parents aspire to the top two tiers of secondary education for their children, the bottom tier becomes increasingly a refuge for immigrants. There is no doubt that in this process, school choice makes some contribution to social polarisation in Haarlem.

Case Study 2

Bradford
Choice in an ethnically diverse English city

Bradford is a socially and ethnically diverse city in the north of England (population 460 000), an industrial-revolution town built on textiles, whose South-Asian immigrant populations account for some 26 per cent of schoolchildren. All state schools in Bradford are comprehensive, in that they accept every kind of pupil, regardless of ability. But patterns of school attendance appear to be strongly influenced by considerations of both race and class, which interact complexly with geographical factors. Bradford is unusual in the United Kingdom for the high rate of growth in its pupil population, due partly to a high birth rate among Asian families. The number of 13 year-olds, for example, will grow by 7 per cent between 1993 and 1998. Yet there has been no recent expansion of physical school provision (except for the opening of a city technology college). The result is pressure on places in many schools, which arguably makes the availability of school places more of an active issue than the pupil or parent's choice of the school in Bradford.

Issues in Bradford

Factors influencing choice

Bradford has three tiers of school: "first schools" (ages 5-9), "middle schools" (9-13) and "upper schools" (13-18). In the first two tiers, geography appears to be the overwhelming influence on school attendance, with most pupils going to their local first school, which serves as a "feeder" to a middle school. But upper schools serve far less well-defined geographical areas, and choices have been made according to a wider range of factors, particularly under the recent national policy of open enrolment, under which clear booklets on "Choosing a school in Bradford" have been issued by the local education authority. Among the factors, other than geography, perceived to influence choices are:

– *Perceptions of school quality,* influenced recently by the publication of "league tables" of examination results.
– *Issues of religion and gender separation* – of particular importance in the case of Muslim girls. The two girls' upper schools in the Bradford state system do not come close to satisfying this demand, the more so because one of them is

Catholic, with a policy of admitting only a minority from non-Catholic families. Any attempt to increase this supply, however, would raise the awkward and common problem that boys' schools are less popular. The local authority is broadly sympathetic to the long-standing possibility of bringing a private Muslim school into the public system, but the stringent requirements of the United Kingdom's national curriculum, among other factors, have made it difficult to bring the school to required standards.

– *Issues of class and race*. Although Bradford's Whites and Asians live together in relative harmony, the issue of race and schooling has always been an emotive one. Some Whites certainly shun inner-city schools that are predominantly Asian, and their behaviour compounds the concentration. But informed observers point out that distinctions between different Asian groups and between different social classes among both Whites and Asians are at least as important as straight White-Brown divisions. One inner-city school with a poor reputation with about 80 per cent Asian pupils is shunned by middle-class Asians and Whites alike. Another, on the edge of the built-up area, has recently enhanced its reputation through strong leadership, and pulls pupils evenly from a wide range of ethnic and income groups.

Allocation of places

A few less popular Bradford schools had surplus places in 1993, but the pressure of rising pupil populations meant that many had to turn away applicants. Schools that are over-subscribed allocated places according to the local authority policy, first giving places to pupils with brothers and sisters already in the school and then to those living closest to the school.

Since the introduction of open enrolment in the 1980s, there has been successively a raising of hopes of greater choice of school, and disappointment that preferences cannot always be met. For example, many inner-city families have applied for upper schools in the mainly white, middle-class Aire Valley area to the north-west of the city, which is well served by bus routes from central Bradford. But as these schools became more popular, they had to narrow their geographical intake to the local area. The proportion of parents not getting their first choice of school (17 per cent in 1992) almost certainly underestimates the reality, as people do not bother applying for schools where they have no realistic chance of getting a place. Perhaps a better indicator of the degree of frustration is the sharp increase in the number of appeals against school allocation; in 1993, there were between 80 and 100 appeals in each of the three upper schools in the Aire Valley.

Schools' response to choice: an example

Despite the fact that only a handful of schools in Bradford are at risk of having unfilled places, most have become much more image-conscious in recent years. In particular, they have tried to portray themselves as solid, reliable schools providing a safe, stable environment. Perhaps the most tangible indicator of this response has been a remarkable change in uniform policies. In the late 1980s, roughly half of schools specified uniform or dress code; by 1993, local officials could not think of a single school that did not have one. In some cases, this change had been requested by the students themselves – from a desire to be in a school that is well regarded from the outside. As uniforms became more common, any school without one tended to have an unfavourable, "scruffy" image.

Opting out

Relatively few Bradford schools have taken the option introduced in 1988 to "opt out" of local authority control. Most that have done so have been upper schools – about 10 per cent of students were in "grant-maintained" schools in this sector by 1993. Interestingly, the most over-subscribed schools have remained under local authority control. But some grant-maintained schools have used their independence to help define their student populations more selectively than might otherwise be possible (see the last two examples below).

Four school examples

- *Pollard Park* middle school serves a community in inner Bradford populated mainly by Asians from India, Pakistan and Bangladesh. Nearly 90 per cent of its 600 pupils are Asian. Some white and Sikh families with high aspirations choose a more racially-balanced middle school for children living in the area, but the great majority attending the local "first school" continue on to Pollard Park. The school tailors its identity to that clientele, giving strong support to Asian families who use it (for example with on-the-spot interpreters), and emphasizing a strict uniform policy. In 1993 it had 157 applicants for 150 places.
- *Ilkley Grammar* school (the term "grammar" given to many Bradford upper schools does not imply selection by ability) is a well-liked neighbourhood school, in an isolated geographical position with its intake largely determined by attendance of "feeder" middle schools. Its outstanding performance in the first examination "league tables" in 1992 threatens, perversely, to disturb this situation with not entirely welcome results. An increase in applications from further afield has led to a higher admission level and greater pressure on places. Ilkley's head teacher considers that the school has insufficient space to cater for its "standard" intake (the number of pupils it is obliged to accept). He also worries that people applying from further afield who get places in the school may eventually, through the rule giving priority to their siblings, force the school to deny places to pupils from its "feeder" middle schools.
- *Bingley Grammar* school, another popular school with a close link to an outlying small town, is also faced with the problem of providing for all those in the area who apply for places. But it has used its status initially as a "voluntary-aided" school (with funding and control shared between a charitable foundation and the local authority) and more recently as a grant-maintained school (having opted out of all local authority control) to define its intake more choosily. Pupils living in Bingley, a community defined by now-redundant borough boundaries, have absolute priority, regardless of siblings or other special factors claimed by those outside. As a grant-maintained school, Bingley Grammar has used financial flexi-

bility to avoid staff cuts faced by surrounding schools and to build a new sports hall, both of which add to its appeal.

– *Thornton Grammar* school opted out of local authority control early in 1993. Its motives were mainly financial – it felt that it had been getting an unfair share of local authority resources. But the first significant change on becoming grant-maintained was to alter its admissions policy, to give priority to people who put it first on their list of choices. This rather controversial policy, in a school with 300 first-choice applicants for 240 places, is designed to restrict intake to those who show a strong commitment to the school.

Commentary

Greater choice of school in Bradford has not led to any radical innovation among local authority and grant-maintained schools. Rather, it has made all schools more conscious of their image, and to look for ways of consolidating their "home" markets. Since central government funding procedures have not allowed these schools to expand or multiply despite overall rising rolls, while there are spare places at some Bradford schools the greatest pressure has been on these less popular schools to attract pupils. In some superficial aspects such as uniform policy, this seems to be making schools more similar, but there is no particular evidence that it has a profound impact on educational standards at the weaker schools. Insofar as it affects school behaviour, it appears to do so in a relatively conservative direction. According to one inner-city head teacher, this is because the strongest pressure comes from aspiring parents (especially Asians) who see education as a route to success for their children, and therefore put traditional objectives such as passing examinations before "humanistic" aims such as creating well-rounded individuals.

Case Study 3

Kent

Student selection in a competitive environment *(England)*

This case study looks at secondary school choice in the county of Kent, one of England's largest local education authorities, and specifically at competition between schools in one of its main towns, Maidstone.

Kent is unusual among English education authorities for two reasons: it is one of a minority where a substantial proportion of secondary schools have taken advantage of the 1988 legislation allowing schools to opt out of local government control, and it is one of the few that retain a system of grammar schools (which select 25 per cent of 11 year-olds by academic ability). On both counts it is interesting as a possible harbinger of the future for elsewhere in England. Even though a general return to grammar schools seems unlikely, there is already evidence to suggest that the selection of pupils in various ways will become increasingly common under England's new "choice" policies.[82] In the international context, Kent's experience is relevant as an example of the atomising of educational decision-making and of the relationship between school selection of pupils and pupils' selection of school.

By mid-1993, a third of secondary schools (but only 1 per cent of primary schools) in Kent had opted to become "grant-maintained" rather than controlled by the local authority. Along with the devolution of management responsibilities to local schools, of which Kent was a pioneer, this has greatly intensified competition among all schools, and to some extent changed its terms. Some grant-maintained non-grammar schools, for example, have tried for the first time to compete for able as well as less able pupils. But in practice, neither the range of choices available nor the status order of schools that determines these choices have so far altered substantially.

Two other factors have been particularly important in the Kent context. One is transport, which is often a constraining factor in choosing schools in a non-metropolitan county with a two-track system of secondary education. The other is politics. Kent was controlled by a Conservative majority for over a century until May 1993, when local elections gave no party overall control. The Conservatives' rule was characterised by strong commitment to the grammar school system and by relatively low spending on education (measured against central government estimates of local need). The change in the council's political colour appears to have come too late for any major change in strategic direction, as much of the local authority's ability to plan secondary education has given way to choices made by schools, parents and pupils. (The scope for a strategic local authority role in primary, nursery and special needs provision remains potentially greater; but this case study focuses on the secondary sector.)

Issues in Kent

Selection of pupils

In most parts of Kent, grammar schools select pupils who pass a test of academic ability at the age of 11. The test is optional, and those who do not sit it, or who fail it, attend a secondary modern school. A small minority of schools, mainly "voluntary-aided" Catholic schools, are comprehensive (*i.e.* they admit children of all abilities). Conversion to a fully comprehensive school system, which had occurred in most other English authorities by the late 1970s, was resisted by the Conservatives in Kent. The Labour and Liberal Democrat parties, which between them gained a majority of seats on the council in 1993, would prefer a comprehensive system. But that would be difficult to introduce, since grammar schools could opt out to retain their status. The result is that the most important choice in secondary schooling in Kent remains the selection of pupils for the grammar school system.

Secondary schools opting out (to become "grant-maintained" schools)

The most common reason for secondary schools to opt out of Kent's control appears to have been dissatisfaction with treatment by the local authority, in particular on financial matters. Schools perceive that they will be able to use resources more flexibly if they control them themselves, and in particular that money spent on centrally provided services will go further when transferred to the individual school – especially under the formula determining grant-maintained schools' revenue, which is regarded as favourable. Some schools have opted out to reposition themselves in the market – as described in the Maidstone examples below.

Funding of schools

This is a key issue in Kent closely related to that of opting out. Some schools that have remained within the system believe that the local authority has become more responsive to their needs as a result of the threat of opt-out. The new political make-up of the council is thought likely to cause proportionately more resources to be devoted to education. But there are two balancing pressures. One is the overall cut in the council's budget, caused by central government policies. The second is the growing difficulty of providing good central services as more schools leave the system, and economies of scale are reduced. This factor could potentially cause opting out to snowball until all schools are grant-maintained.

Competition among schools

Competition of all types has increased dramatically under the pressures of pupil-based resources and open enrolment. Brochures have become glossy, open-evening programmes have become increasingly extensive, and advertising by many schools in the press has been outdone by some grant-maintained schools' advertising on television. Some schools have changed their names to make themselves sound more respectable, for example from "high school" to "community college" and from "Clare Park" (the name of a public housing estate) to "The Malling School". Teachers have been encouraged to "sell" the school's image actively, and some schools have appointed press liaison officers to let newspapers know of their successes.

Transport

This is a crucial factor in determining school choice in Kent, not just because of its many rural districts, but also because of its grammar school system. Since grammar schools select only one in four children, their "catchment" areas are on average four times the size of a comprehensive secondary school of the same size. This consideration is made more important by the rules determining access to free school transport for those living over three miles away from their "nearest appropriate school". This creates a predisposition in such cases for parents on modest incomes to send children to the closest grammar or secondary modern school, and makes other choices available mainly to the better-off.

Maidstone's market

In Maidstone, a town of 86 000 people which is Kent's administrative centre, competition has been especially intense, influenced in particular by two local factors. First, in the mid-Kent area which includes Maidstone, it is likely that one or two secondary schools will have to close because of overprovision. Secondly, a significant change in the secondary school system took effect in 1993. Testing for grammar school entry had previously taken place at age 13, after two years in which all students were mixed together at "high schools" for 11-16 year-olds. These schools were able to retain some able pupils after age 13. The system change which brought forward the test and grammar school entry to the age of 11, as in most of Kent, effectively downgraded the high schools to "secondary moderns" with only the less able pupils. Schools have looked for ways of escaping the inferior image that goes with this status.

Examples of school responses:

- The **Maplesden Noakes School** is one of six high schools in mid-Kent (of a total of 13) that have opted out to try to avoid becoming schools for less able pupils only under the policy described in the previous paragraph. Effectively, these schools are trying to become comprehensive, not an easy task where selective grammar schools exist nearby. A crucial factor is the creation of a "sixth form" – provision for 16-18 year-olds which in grammar schools are seen as a key symbol of academic excellence. Only two of the six schools – including Maplesden Noakes – have had central government permission to create a sixth form. (Despite a theoretically *laissez-faire* attitude towards grant-maintained schools, the Department for Education is aware that some changes of character necessitate capital spending, and is wary of overprovision.) The problem for Maplesden Noakes has been the circular one of attracting enough able pupils to sustain a sixth form offering a good range of courses, and thus attract more able pupils. But the attention paid to its academic image has perhaps helped Maplesden Noakes to consolidate a more general advantage – that it is seen as the most "middle-class" of the non-grammar schools in the area, an advantage helped by its location in an affluent part of Maidstone. This has helped it to attract applications in excess of available places.

– *The Astor of Hever School* is a high school that has remained with the local authority and adopted a very different strategy from Maplesden Noakes, its nearby competitor. It sees itself as setting realistic goals in relation to a mixed social intake that excludes the most able pupils. It aims to provide a solid education in an environment that stresses basic values, from age 11 to 16, and to direct pupils to options in other schools and colleges thereafter. It does its best to demonstrate its character and ethos to its customers; for three days every October, the school opens its doors to parents, who can observe classrooms in session. Its brochure is informative rather than glossy. Yet this "solid" strategy failed dramatically in market terms in 1993, the first year in which grammar schools were also competing for 11 year-olds. Astor of Hever attracted only 95 pupils for 150 places. Maplesden Noakes effectively won the battle for a limited clientele, with a more up-market image.

– *Maidstone Grammar School for Girls* has had no need to adapt its image or its marketing strategy in response to competition. Its outstanding examination results in the first "league tables", published in 1992, confirmed a reputation that has caused some families to move to the area from London to get their children places. But although Maidstone Girls is over-subscribed, its headmistress would not (unlike some popular grammar school heads) wish to select from a still narrower band of ability than the prescribed 25 per cent, preferring to work within a planned system that sets a common test. But she fears that this system might be breaking down, with schools opting out and a declining support structure from the centre.

– *Oakwood Park Grammar School*, a boys' school that has opted out, appears to be using its flexibility to become less selective rather than more so. One of four grammar schools in mid-Kent, it has had problems attracting enough qualified pupils from those who pass the standard test, so has been accepting up to 25 per cent of its intake from pupils of lower assessed ability. This is a questionable policy under the school's approved admission regulations. It also causes the complication that those who have not passed the selection test are not eligible for free transport to grammar schools. But such a policy could be a precursor of entry requirements set by individual schools rather than a system-wide definition of the difference between "grammar" and "secondary modern".

Commentary

The desirability of Kent schools tends to be judged mainly along the single dimension of perceived academic quality, corresponding to the judgements of pupils' academic quality, made at the age of 11. These judgements are clearer than ever with the help of published "league tables" of academic results. A social dimension in terms of the backgrounds of pupils in a school is also important, but tends to correlate fairly closely with the academic dimension. The schools observed do not appear as yet to have found ways of offering particular educational advantages that effectively cut across these criteria for choosing.

Case Study 4

Stockholm
Competition between schools
in the Järva school district *(Sweden)*

Since 1991, pupils in Stockholm have been allowed to enrol in any school, not just their nearest one, with money following pupils. A minority of pupils (about 10 per cent in the first year) have taken advantage of this option, but in some cases this has had a significant impact on schools. One of the more striking cases of local competition is between three schools in the Järva district of North Stockholm. A less popular school, in an area with a high immigrant population, has been losing pupils to two neighbouring schools with a greater proportion of Swedish origin pupils. As a result, all three schools have put more effort into marketing, and the less popular school has taken steps to try to improve its programmes.

The schools

All schools are grades 7-9 (ages 13-16):
- *Husby* school has 241 pupils, two-thirds of them immigrants, in a poor area with 95 per cent of families living in rented flats, and many receiving social support. A considerable number of refugees have recently moved to the area here. The school is important to the area as the only firm point of reference for many families.
- *Åkalla* school has 333 pupils, one-third of them immigrants, in an area with a somewhat more balanced social mix than Husby's neighbourhood, but still densely populated with many people living in flats.
- *Ärvinge* school has 420 pupils, one-third of them immigrants, in an area of terraced houses and co-operatively owned flats where most parents are in good jobs.

The policy

From school year 1991/92, in advance of the rest of Sweden, Stockholm introduced an open enrolment policy, which permits pupils to enrol in a school other than their assigned local one, and distributes about 50 per cent of money for schools on a per-pupil basis. This creates a direct financial incentive for schools with classes that are not full to attract extra pupils, who in such cases bring with them more money than the marginal cost of teaching them.

Examples of outcomes

Husby has been losing pupils from its catchment area. In 1993, 24 of these pupils opted for grade 7 in the other two schools, representing about a quarter of Husby's normal intake. In practice, migration into the area meant that the reduction in pupil numbers was only 11, but since much of this migration occurred after the finances were calculated, the school lost revenue equivalent to 20 pupils. The school has had to shed four or five teachers, although this is largely due to general budget cuts.

Husby's response to this situation has been to seek general educational improvements to make its school more attractive. It has developed better co-ordination with other levels of compulsory school in the area. The principal has drawn up a specific improvement plan.

Three-quarters of the pupils lost by Husby went to Åkalla. This has made it possible to create an extra grade 7 class. The school has put stress on marketing from an early stage; parents are informed of developments through a twice-a-term newsletter and regular information meetings.

Ärvinge received five extra pupils from Husby's catchment area, and 17 from another district, Rinkeby-Tensta. This has made it possible to maintain the school with five classes in grade 7.

Segregation appears to be increasing, with immigrants moving into the Husby area, and Swedish origin families moving out.

Commentary

Despite some of the difficulties caused, the head teachers of all three schools tend to see the competition in positive terms. The following are their comments:
- *Husby:* "Competition improves the quality and engagement [of the school]. Marketing is needed to break the trend [of students choosing other schools]."
- *Åkalla:* "It is of great value for a school to be examined. The option must be made consciously and one should make the choice of moving *to* a school, not *from* a school."
- *Ärvinge:* "The development for Ärvinge has been positive. In financial terms it has meant additional contributions. The school has a good reputation which has had a positive effect on all the staff at the school. The percentage of immigrants is high but not too high. The Swedish language dominates."

Case Study 5
Melbourne
Public-private school competition *(Australia)*

How do subsidies to private schools from the Australian Commonwealth and state governments affect the choices available to parents? Do schools in different sectors compete for the same pupils? Do private schools develop their markets at the expense of government schools? The answers to these questions are complex and varied, but can be illustrated by examples of schools in two areas of Melbourne. Waverley is an affluent suburb in the east of the city; Dandenong/Springvale is a much poorer area in the south. Each case considers three secondary schools (mainly ages 12-18) – one government, one Catholic and one other private school.

Waverley

The schools

- *Mount Waverley Secondary College* is a government school with a strong, academically-oriented reputation. It has no problem attracting the 1 400 students who fill its rolls; 30 per cent come from beyond its designated catchment area. Since it is about 10 per cent over-subscribed, it is one of six schools in its region to admit out-of-zone students on an "appeal" basis – exercising various criteria, the main ones being whether applicants have siblings at the school and whether there are particular reasons that they would benefit from the school's curriculum – for example if they are particularly interested in its Japanese programme.

  Like many schools in the area, Mount Waverley actively promotes itself in existing and potential catchment areas, particularly through visits to potential feeder schools. Since there is a significant crossover from public primary into private secondary schools, contact with primaries is one way of persuading children and parents that Mount Waverley can offer a high-quality curriculum to rival that of private schools. There is significant crossover in enrolment between Mount Waverley and private schools at ages 14 and 16 – around 20-40 pupils in each direction at each age.

  The result of a recent merger of two schools, it operates on two sites, but brings senior (17-18 year-old) students together on one site to create a more varied set of options. Another way that it enriches its offerings is by using voluntary parental contributions to enhance such things as music and technology provision. Each parent is asked for A$ 240 a year; around 75 per cent pay it.

- **Avila College** is a girls' Catholic school with 950 pupils. It offers a balanced secondary curriculum and puts particular stress on pastoral care and the development of each individual student. The school's fees range from A$ 1 650 to 1 812, and are supplemented, like in other Catholic schools, by government subsidies providing the majority of income. Avila follows the Catholic philosophy of not excluding any pupils who cannot afford to pay, and in a number of cases fees are waived or reduced.

  The great majority of students come to Avila from Catholic primary schools. When falling rolls in the 1980s produced a shortfall of pupils from the school's main feeder primaries, it recruited from Catholic schools over a wider area. There is thus limited competition with other sectors, although the assignment of a staff member to public relations duties is a sign of the school's awareness of the need to develop its constituency.

- **Wesley College** is a highly prestigious, co-educational independent school with about 3 000 students over three campuses, including some primary school children. With a rich curriculum and very good facilities, its enrolment is determined to a large extent by those who can afford its fees of up to A$ 8 000 a year, but also by preference for its relatively liberal, Christian philosophy and by space: there is a long time-ordered waiting list. The college receives a small proportion of its income from the Commonwealth government, according to the least generous category of its grant scale. Most parents of Wesley pupils have a predisposition towards private schools, and often it is financial affordability that is the main criterion for choice – a number of pupils have had to leave as the result of the effect of recession on parents, a large proportion of whom are in private business.

Commentary

To a large extent, parents in Waverley make choices within three sectors – public, Catholic and other private – rather than between them. But competition at the margins is important, and appears to be increasing.

Catholic parents are reported to be concerned more directly than in the past with educational quality as a criterion for choice, and Catholic schools respond by participating where possible in curriculum development being undertaken in the public sector. Avila for example has joined in efforts to develop senior studies that combine technical and further education (TAFE) with the normal secondary school-leaving certificate.

In hard economic times, public secondary schools such as Mount Waverley have an incentive to show to financially pressed private school parents that they can imitate the strengths of private schools within a free system. Schools such as Wesley have not so far felt threatened by such competition, but see the possibility of change on the horizon. One of Wesley's campus principals observes that public secondary school mergers have already reduced the difference in terms of facilities and curriculum diversity between the best public and the best private schools. The next critical stage, she believes, would be for principals to gain more management responsibility for their schools, particularly in selecting staff. The "Schools of the Future" programme has been introduced by the Victoria government with precisely that objective.

Dandenong/Springvale

The schools

- *Maranatha Christian School* is an independent school whose rolls grew from 97 when it opened in 1971 to 750 in 1993. It serves a "pocket-sized" middle-class area surrounded by working-class areas with high unemployment. The school receives 50 per cent of its income from Commonwealth and state government grants. It charges A$ 5 094 a year per family, for all children attending the school, which runs from age 5 to age 18. The headmaster believes that generous government support enables many parents to choose his school in preference to a government school.

  The school requires pupils to come from Protestant Christian homes, and discourages Catholic, Seventh Day Adventist, Jehovah's Witness and Church of the Latter Day Saints families. Its curriculum is similar to that of government schools, but the school distinguishes itself by a stress on high standards of behaviour and Christian teaching. The school does not advertise, relying on word of mouth for publicity. In the recession of the early 1990s, a fall in enrolments contributed to financial difficulties. Although Maranatha has a policy of assisting parents in financial difficulties, it had to ask three families to remove their children because of non-payment of fees in 1992.

- *Doveton Secondary College* is a government school with 540 students, many of whom have recently enrolled as a result of two others closing in the area. Situated in a suburb that is part of the poorest socio-economic area of Melbourne, it was classed as a technical school until 1991, and had a poor reputation. Latterly it has been trying to promote itself as a new progressive secondary college. In 1993 it received a substantial grant to repair and refurbish its buildings, which were in urgent need of maintenance. Unlike many Australian schools, it does not ask parents to make financial contributions.

  There are no zoning restrictions applying to enrolment at the school, which actively engages in cross-age tutoring, curriculum development and other activities with the local primary schools from which it recruits pupils. It advertises in the local press, and invites every local parent with a child about to enter secondary school to meet the principal and view the college. Some students are attracted from further afield by Doveton College's reputation as the district's science and technology centre. It also has an innovative and successful programme of preparation for the school-leaving certificate. It hopes to attract some students from the independent and, to a lesser degree, Catholic sector as its image improves and more families feel the effects of the recession. It is one of the pilot schools in the state government's "Schools of the Future" devolution programme, and uses this fact in advertising.

- *Killester College* is a girls' Catholic school in Springvale, another poor suburb. Its 788 students are charged A$ 1 400, but helped by government subsidies the school claims not to exclude any student who cannot pay. This has created severe financial pressure on the school following the closure of nearby factories.

Killester does not offer as broad a curriculum as Doveton Secondary College, but does not advertise for students as it is the only all-girls' Catholic school in the district. A drop in the number of students entering the school in 1993 caused it to close one of its classes. The school is dismissive of the effect the government self-managing schools will have on its numbers, and is not worried about competition from independent schools. It believes that Catholic parents will continue to enrol their children in the school for its religious content, strict discipline and pastoral care. Its explanation for the drop in enrolments is that parents have left the area seeking employment. It remains to be seen whether its confidence in retaining the loyalty of those who stay will be justified.

Commentary

In this depressed working-class area, many families who would see a "private" education as desirable for their children cannot afford that option. Small independent schools like Maranatha are at greater risk of losing students to government schools like Doveton Secondary College as it improves its image and gets greater flexibility, through devolution, to resource programmes that are responsive to student needs. Small independent schools, on the other hand, would need to raise their fees to extend their programmes, and this might risk driving some parents away. Catholic schools in the area feel relatively secure because of their special religious character, but this could be misplaced if government schools are able to offer significantly superior curricula, and start marketing themselves more like private schools.

Conclusion

The State of Victoria has a long and entrenched history of private education, with a marked delineation between non-government and government schools. But those government schools that flourish under local management may in future be in a better position to compete with the private sector. The pressure will then increase for non-government schools to show that they can offer students something different that provides a good return for their fees.

Case Study 6
Specialised schools in New South Wales *(Australia)*

Since the late 1980s, a right-of-centre state government has been departing from the model of a single comprehensive secondary school in New South Wales. In particular, it has created three kinds of school: some specialising in specific subject areas, some selecting children by ability and some offering a particular style of education to 17 and 18 year-olds only. These innovations have been associated on the one hand with "dezoning" of schools with the aim of giving greater choice, and on the other with attempts to improve the quality of schooling through the development of particular subjects in the state-wide curriculum and through better links with other stages of education. Choice in New South Wales has therefore been introduced in the context of managed improvement in education rather than being a pure *laissez-faire* policy.

Characteristics

- *Schools have been "dezoned" since 1990,* in the sense that rules compelling children to attend the school nearest their home have been abolished. However, where schools are over-subscribed, priority has almost always been according to closeness to the school.
- *A range of specialised high schools (ages 12-18) has been introduced,* most notably in languages (17 schools) and technology (28 schools). Most have been redesignated from being comprehensive schools, although some are new buildings. Specialised high schools create curriculum diversity in addition to the strong core curriculum being developed by the state authorities. Language schools offer three foreign languages, and are seen both as useful indicators of demand for language study (found to be high) and as models in language teaching for other schools. Technology schools offer a fully comprehensive curriculum but use and foster an understanding of new technologies in all areas of study, and play an active role in the development of the state's technology curriculum. Specialised schools are designated on a geographically well-distributed basis to provide even access.
- *Some high schools have been designated as "selective",* accepting students strictly on the basis of performance in a state-wide test of academic ability. The 19 selective high schools in operation by 1994 had place for roughly 5 per cent of children entering secondary schools in New South Wales. These schools aim to create a challenging environment for gifted pupils. In 1993 over 14 000 applicants

applied for 3 000 places at these schools. Some specialist schools also select by ability, including music, performing arts and agricultural high schools.
- *Some schools are being converted into "senior colleges" for the final two years of high school.* The aim is to offer a choice of more flexible and accredited pathways between schools, technical and further education (TAFE) colleges and tertiary institutions such as universities. These institutions have also been associated with an effort to improve the retention of pupils in education until year 12 (age 18). The retention rate has risen from 30 per cent in 1979 to 56 per cent in 1991.

Background/evolution

From the 1960s onwards, a divide between technical and general education was abolished and most (although not all) schools that had been selective stopped being so. The uniform comprehensive system that emerged was seen as grossly inappropriate by the Conservative government that came to power in New South Wales in 1988. The preceding Labour administration had introduced limited diversity by starting a performing arts high school and a music conservatory. But the new government set out more systematically to offer alternatives to comprehensive schools across the state. The declared objective was not to destroy the notion of a comprehensive school, but to create competition and models of excellence in certain curriculum areas that would encourage comprehensive schools to improve.

Examples of outcomes

Specialised schools, senior colleges and in particular selective schools have proved popular choices. Whether they can demonstrate the improvement of standards that is expected of them has not yet been fully assessed. The six-year high school cycle, ending in a school-leaving examination, creates a long evaluation period for high school reform. Early indications do not show an unequivocal rise in pupil results in these schools.

The following are examples of schools, all in Sydney, in each of the three categories described above:

- *Cherrybrook Technology High School* is a purpose-built technology school, with state-of-the-art equipment supplied by a range of corporate partners, notably IBM. This school uses technology creatively to help pupils become independent learners. It would like to select pupils over a wide area according to aptitude, but may not refuse any applicant within a local zone defined by the state authorities. The school has proved so popular that in 1993 it had only ten places available to non-local pupils, 160 of whom applied. The desire to buy homes in the catchment area has led local estate agents to advertise its existence as far afield as Hong Kong, to attract families moving to Australia.

The school is seen as a "lighthouse" of technology excellence. But in sharp contrast to England's city technology colleges (see Case Study 7), it systematically spreads its light to other public schools. In 1992, it had no fewer than

200 visits from outside groups, three-quarters of them teachers from other schools. It also offered in-service courses for teachers on other sites, and sold teaching time to primary schools.

As a new school, Cherrybrook is well placed to use technology in imaginative new ways. Schools that have been redesignated as technology schools by the state government do not always do so. According to one observer, the most common reaction is a "cargo cult" mentality – a worship of the extra hardware without changing the school's fundamental way of operating. A minority of schools react to redesignation with detailed discussions among teachers of implications for classroom practice.

– *St. Mary's Senior High School* was an ordinary high school until 1988, when it became the state's first "senior college". Its atmosphere is somewhere between a college campus and a secondary school, combining the adult freedoms associated with the former with the pastoral care of the latter. This combination attracted 700 applicants for 400 places in 1993, with some travelling up to an hour to reach the school. Thirty pupils are adults. Students are able to take courses giving credit in the technical and further education system, to study part-time, and to control their own timetable. The school has improved its retention rate by putting a high stress on mentoring and counselling. About 30 per cent of entrants to St. Mary's are attracted there from independent schools.

– *Penrith Selective High School* is situated in a commercial area of a working-class suburb in the west of Sydney. The main reason for its redesignation as a selective school in 1989 was local demographic decline: by attracting pupils from over a wider area, the school was able to stay open. Its rolls declined from 1 100 students in 1986 to 760 in 1992. By 1993, about 1 100 children were applying to enter the school's seventh grade alone. Redesignation did not immediately lead to changes in the school's style, even though it dramatically changed its intake. Rather, change was evolutionary, with staff taking courses on teaching gifted children.

One effect of the redesignation has been to encourage surrounding schools to attempt to make themselves more attractive to gifted children; another is to make independent schools feel that there is serious competition from the public sector. But the small numbers of pupils entering selective schools in New South Wales (5 per cent) means that the risk of comprehensive schools being disadvantaged by the creaming-off of their brightest pupils is limited. In contrast, British grammar schools traditionally accepted 20-25 per cent of children. If such schools do not continue indefinitely to expand, therefore, they may with some justification be seen as "lighthouse" examples for the teaching of gifted children, just as technology and language schools are lighthouses. The problem, however, is that the existence of selective schools has generated intense demand from a wider section of the population, whose hopes of attending them are being confounded by the narrowness of the intake. There is therefore pressure to expand to the point where they seriously threaten the capacity of schools to be "comprehensive".

Commentary

In New South Wales, policies for choice have been related closely to specific educational objectives. The creation of diverse choices is therefore aiming to enrich educational possibilities across the system, rather than simply to create a set of options for the chosen. An emerging problem is that the popularity of the special options, which are not universally, means that they are not available to all who desire them. To reduce the frustration that this creates, one of two things might eventually have to happen: either the reputations of comprehensive schools will have to be improved to compete with those of specialised schools, or the idea of comprehensive schools will have to be abandoned, with every school acquiring some special defining character.

Case Study 7

City Technology Colleges[83] *(England)*

At the initiative of central government, 15 "city technology colleges" (CTCs) have been established mainly in relatively deprived areas of English cities. This new model of secondary school aims to deliver an innovative, technologically-oriented education to children from a wide range of social backgrounds and ability groups, who share with their families a commitment to the school and its goals. Sponsored by private business and run by independent trusts, CTCs nevertheless have all their running costs and a portion of their capital paid by central government.

The development of different CTCs has varied considerably, often owing more to local circumstances than to centrally-defined objectives for this "sector". However, most do offer a distinctive alternative to nearby schools. But this choice is available only to a small proportion of pupils, even in the areas that the schools serve. All but one of the CTCs have to turn away more pupils than they enrol.

Characteristics

City technology colleges are:
- *sponsored* by private businesses, which provide part of the initial capital to create the school, and are associated with its development. In most cases a main sponsor is closely identified with the school, sometimes through its name;
- *governed* by bodies set up by the sponsors under funding agreements for each college. They are run without government interference, and are exempted from many regulations covering maintained schools;
- *financed* for their running costs by grants from central government based on a calculation of how much is spent per pupil in ordinary schools in similar areas. Capital costs are shared by government and sponsors, but the original aim of companies paying most or all of these costs has not been achieved. Government paid about 80 per cent of the initial capital costs of 15 CTCs, at a public cost of over £100 million;
- *distinctive* in a variety of ways, depending on the school. Extra emphasis on technology and applied subjects in the curriculum is an important element in most schools, but does not always represent the most important or radical break with normal school practice. A longer school day, and high stress on using information technology, made possible by an ample supply of computers, are usually central

features. A commitment to provide a coherent education from age 11 to 18 for all pupils, rather than expecting many pupils to leave school at 16, is a common objective, yet to be fully tested;
- *over-subscribed* in terms of pupil applications. In 1991, there were between 4.4 and 1.8 times as many applicants as places at the CTCs in operation;
- *required to admit* a group of pupils from across the ability range and representative of the community in the catchment area. The latter is hard to apply precisely but seems to prevent CTCs' student intakes from becoming obviously unbalanced in these terms; expected to use *aptitude* and *motivation* as criteria for selection: schools seek children who are suited and committed to an education with a technological bias. Since aptitude at age 11 can be hard to assess, this creates a highly discretionary basis for choosing pupils. In many cases, interviews of pupils and parents are crucial.

Background/evolution

City technology colleges were announced in 1986 as a means of providing an alternative choice of school to children living in inner-city areas. The political assumption behind this announcement was that schools run by local authorities had failed to meet the needs of many pupils living in these areas, and that CTCs would be "beacons of excellence" demonstrating how a different kind of school was possible. The later announcement that any school would be allowed to opt out of local authority control outshadowed CTCs in terms of one objective – to break the local government monopoly on education. But the CTC idea remained distinctive in terms of industrial sponsorship, wide catchment areas and the technological character of the schools.

Originally, 20 CTCs were planned by 1990. Difficulties in finding sponsors caused this number to be reduced, and an abandoning of the aim that most original capital should come from the sponsors. Many large companies were reluctant to get involved with a controversial initiative that helped only a few schools, at a time when they were attempting to establish partnerships with many ordinary schools across the country.

In these circumstances, each CTC that was established relied on a particular local situation rather than a central government masterplan. Several early sponsors were successful, maverick entrepreneurs with a strong local base, rather than large established corporations. The location of CTCs was determined to a large degree by the identification of suitable sites. Only some ended up in the particularly deprived inner-city areas originally identified by the government, although all cater for at least some poorer urban districts.

In 1992, the Department for Education proposed that the idea of "technology colleges" should be extended to include any grant-maintained school or "voluntary-aided" school (run by religious and other foundations and mainly funded by local authorities) that wished to specialise in technology and met certain criteria including a partnership with business sponsors.

Examples of outcomes

The impact of the CTC initiative is hard to assess, given the range of practices that have emerged in the different schools. The following outcomes may however be observed:
- *The "beacon" effect of these schools has been limited* by their tendency not to be seen as part of a wider "system". In some cases, the schools are run by dedicated educators who see them as a good environment to try out new ideas. Despite the affiliation of some 60 schools to the trust that promotes CTCs, the potential for spreading the lessons learned from these experiments is limited by the lack of established networks involving CTCs and other schools, and in some cases by hostility to this sector from local authorities.
- *The special character of CTCs has not created a single coherent new approach to teaching technology,* but has demonstrated in many cases the potential for extensive use of computers throughout the curriculum. But the cost of maintaining such a system, with running costs linked to those of ordinary public schools, makes CTC directors feel less financially privileged than they are often regarded by outsiders.
- *The traditional English definition of academic excellence competes in CTCs* with their mission to create a new kind of excellence. In their formative years, CTCs were highly sensitive to parental values, and many did not wish to seem excessively focused on science and technology at the expense of other subjects. The result is sometimes an odd mixture of innovation and traditionalism – typified by a CTC director who marches round his high-tech premises admonishing pupils who contravene the school dress code.
- *City technology colleges are chosen for a variety of reasons,* of which emphasis on technology is only one. Interviews with parents and pupils at two CTCs[84] were influenced by a variety of factors, including the perception that CTCs were something "new and different", the publicity the schools had got in particular for their good equipment, and the perception that they would be "the next best thing to a grammar school". A common misapprehension, that CTCs select more clever pupils, is fed by the setting of tests to applicants – necessary in order to meet the requirement of accepting pupils from a wide ability range.

Commentary

City technology colleges have undoubtedly provided a previously unavailable choice to many pupils. By ensuring that neither high academic achievement nor high social status gives undue access, they offer this choice to some pupils whose educational chances would otherwise have been limited. By often attracting pupils from a wide geographical area, they much reduce the risk of harming any one neighbourhood school by attracting the most highly-motivated pupils.

The most obvious limitation of CTCs is their small number. They are only available to a minority of those who would like to benefit, even in the areas where they operate. This would be less of a concern if CTCs had a tangible impact on the education system more widely. But a crucial feature of CTCs is that they behave more like enterprises and less like institutions than most schools, and seem to put a priority on results for their own "business" rather than on "system benefits". Private innovation may, of course, be copied by competitors. The new possibility of creating "technology colleges" from ordinary schools is designed to allow that to happen. The degree to which such diversity spreads in English secondary schooling will therefore be an important determinant of the eventual impact of CTCs. However, some of their characteristics, most notably the advantages of millions of pounds' worth of public and private start-up capital, together with plenty of free publicity, are unlikely to be duplicated.

Case Study 8

Wieselgrensskolan
A "profile" school in Helsingborg *(Sweden)*

This comprehensive school (ages 7-16) has taken advantage of a liberalisation of rules to create specialised programmes focusing on music and in football, and thus to attract pupils from beyond its normal catchment area. This has created extra competition within the system in accordance with the objectives of the municipality, though under relatively controlled conditions.

Characteristics

The 550-pupil school has opened an extra class from the fourth grade (age 10) onwards, specialising in music, and another from the seventh grade (age 13) specialising in football. In each case, pupils follow a curriculum with extra classes in the specialised subject. Their contemporaries in other classes follow an ordinary curriculum, but derive some benefit from the strengthening of the school in the two subjects. Where demand for places outstrip supply, pupils are selected according to ability in the area of specialisation.

Background/evolution

The municipality granted the necessary permission to the school to vary its curriculum from the 1992/93 school year, after a complex application process. Profile schools are in line with Helsingborg's policy of enhancing the operation of markets and choice. A survey of this new policy in applications for places in school year 1993/94 showed that fewer than 2 per cent of pupils applied for schools outside their catchment area – but the most common reason for doing so (other than living on the border of the catchment area) was to go to a "special interest" or "profile" school.

Examples of outcomes

In the first year of operation, 50 pupils applied for the music class. Thirty were accepted. This created a higher ratio of pupils to teachers than in other classes, effectively earning the school money under the new budgetary regime that allows greater flexibility to schools over both spending priorities and class size. The school's average class size is 25, but a class of 30 selected, well-motivated students is thought to be easily manageable. Budgetary flexibility is used to provide in-service training and to purchase extra music equipment, but there are not major extra costs associated with the programme. The headmaster considers that he has control over about SKr 3 million out of a total budget of SKr 26 million: there is little flexibility as yet in terms of teachers' salaries.

The football programme attracted applications from only 22 pupils in the first year, all of whom were accepted.

In attempting to attract pupils in the fourth grade, often from schools that serve grades 1 to 6, Wieselgrensskolan finds itself in direct competition with these schools. Since it cannot rely on them to let third-grade pupils know of the music option, it mails all these pupils' parents directly.

The music profile of the school appears to have increased parental participation considerably: most music classes have direct parental involvement; once a month, a school conference is held, with parents participating.

Commentary

In a country in which parents are not on the whole inclined to exercise their newly-acquired right to select a school other than the local one to which their children are assigned, any attempt to create a "market" in compulsory schooling probably needs some stimulation. This supply-side attempt to create a greater variety of visible options in the public sector has made a start, by encouraging parents to choose an alternative to the ordinary local school. Although this initiative remains within the framework controlled by the municipal authorities, the school and its principal enjoy a growing flexibility in decision-making, previously unknown in the Swedish context. If support for the music options continue to increase, the principal believes that he would be able to open a second class to meet demand, without having to refer back to the school board that originally gave him authority to specialise.

Case Study 9

Every school a magnet in Montclair, New Jersey *(United States)*

This small town of 40 000 inhabitants 15 miles from New York City has made all of its seven elementary and both of its middle schools into "magnets": each has a distinctive character and all parents may choose from among them, regardless of residence. Since there is a relatively even "status order" among schools, most choices can be met. Parents put a big effort into choosing schools and are heavily involved in everyday school activities. However, there is evidence that poorer parents participate in different ways from middle-class ones.

Characteristics

Montclair school district educated a total of 5 722 pupils in 1992/93, in:
- *seven kindergarten/elementary schools,* delivering a common core curriculum but with the following specialisms/themes: science and technology; "fundamental", *i.e.* focusing on basics (ages 4-11); Montessori/arts; international studies; family involvement; and "gifted/talented" (two schools covering different age ranges);
- *two middle schools (ages 11-14)* specialising in the gifted/talented and science and technology;
- *one comprehensive high school* with no single specialism but optional courses that follow on from some of the middle schools' specialisms.

None of the schools are heavily specialised; rather, their special characteristics represent an element of their ethos. In the "science and technology" elementary school, for example, computers are used as a routine learning tool rather than studied as a subject. The middle school for the "talented and gifted", like its elementary counterparts, does *not* select pupils by ability; its premise is that every pupil is talented in some sphere, basing its philosophy loosely on Howard Gardner's theory of "multiple intelligences". Classes in optional subjects as dance, language and industrial arts attempt to nurture these strengths.

Parents of children from age four may apply to any school, listing up to three choices in preference order. After taking account first of siblings in school and then of balancing races and sexes in each school, selection for over-subscribed schools is random. The school board and each school organise open days; parents are able to talk to principals and observe classes in action before choosing.

Background/evolution

Magnet schools were first introduced in 1977 to help create a more representative racial balance among Montclair schools, which had been ordered by the State Commissioner of Education. Over the course of the 1980s, all Montclair schools became "magnets".

Examples of outcomes

- Over 90 per cent of parents get their children into their first or second choice school. Those who fail to obtain their first choice are given priority if they reapply to the same school the following year, but the majority remain in the school that is allocated.
- The majority of pupils do not attend their closest school; some 80 per cent travel to school by bus.
- There is no clear hierarchy of school preferences. However, the science/technology elementary school, with a strong principal and a dynamic, friendly atmosphere, is over-subscribed by about four to one. The "fundamental" school has fewer applicants than places, and a number of white pupils in particular end up there by forced assignment.
- Less popular schools are not directly penalised in terms of student numbers or money, but ultimately their character is reviewed. Two programmes, on future studies and basic arts, have been scrapped through lack of support; the fundamental school is now being reconsidered.
- A detailed study[85] of how parents in Montclair choose schools revealed two things of particular interest:
  • Parents choose schools more by their general atmosphere than their specialisms. This might partly be because the most significant choice is made for children aged four: each elementary school is considered a "feeder" into a particular middle school, so there is less active choice at this stage.
  • Better-off parents tend to search more thoroughly than poorer parents, backing up hearsay more systematically with written materials and visits to schools. Greater search efforts correlate with greater satisfaction with the choice made.
- Sometimes choice within schools can be more significant than inter-school choice. For example, in the "talented and gifted" middle school, some parents lobby intensely to get children into particular "houses" in order to get them the right teachers. One assertive mother even mailed the principal a box of water that she claimed was her child's tears caused by disappointment at being allocated to the "wrong" house.
- After magnet schools were introduced in Montclair, test scores rose and schools became more racially balanced, according to a 1987 report by the Educational Testing Service. The growth in the proportion of better-off families enrolling children in private schools has been halted.

Commentary

Parental choice of and involvement in Montclair schools appears to contribute positively to their atmosphere and to parents' satisfaction. Low rates of pupil turnover are both a sign of this satisfaction and a potential cause, as it contributes to a stable environment. However, the main impetus behind educational change in Montclair has been supply- rather than demand-driven: decisions taken by educators and school administrators, not parents "voting with their feet", have been the main determinants of new educational offerings. But if a certain set of offerings does not meet parents' approval, this becomes plain to educators, and it is reviewed.

Case Study 10

Kura Kaupapa Maori

New Zealand's support for Maori schools

Since 1989, the original settlers of New Zealand, the Maori, have received public funding to run schools teaching their language and culture. *Kura Kaupapa Maori* means "school(s) with a Maori charter"; by 1993, 23 primary and one secondary *kura* were in operation.

The concept of *kura* is of Maori origin, and the initiative's main aim is to maintain and preserve the Maori language and values. Parents who choose these schools are effectively making a cultural as well as educational choice and commitment, in a society dominated by a European origin culture. The recognition and funding of Maori schools by the Ministry of Education are part of an affirmative action programme designed to enhance Maori education and development, in mainstream as well as separate schools.

Characteristics

- *The key feature of* Kura Kaupapa Maori *is total immersion in the language.* This is deemed necessary, given that English has become the main language used in the home of the great majority of Maori families.
- *Schools teach a curriculum based on Maori values, philosophies, principles and practices.* They are also required to comply with the provisions of the main Education Acts governing other schools.
- *The distinctiveness of the* kura *is preserved by both internal and external disciplines.* The boards that run the schools are committed to the concept of a Maori style of education, set out in a charter. In addition, the Ministry of Education requires that *kura* provide an education of a kind not available at other public schools.
- Kura *are small,* with an average of 60 pupils in the primary schools.
- Kura *have particularly close links with parents,* who have shown a commitment by enrolling their children. In some cases, parents are required to place their children in a pre-school "language nest" in order to obtain a place at a *kura*.
- *The* kura *are funded at the same level as other public schools.* This creates difficulties, because teaching in Maori is so new that there are few ready-made teaching materials, and schools have to develop their own. Maori is traditionally

an oral language. The shortage of qualified Maori-language teachers is also a severe problem.
- *Funding is also available for Maori-language teaching in other New Zealand schools,* although the schools are accused of using their new budgetary autonomy to divert these funds elsewhere. A ten-point plan for Maori education developed in 1991 aims to improve Maori progress in mainstream education as well as providing options for separate Maori initiatives.

Background/evolution

Maoris do not believe they have had a good deal in New Zealand society since the ceding of sovereignty to the British Crown at the Treaty of Waitangi in 1840. The majority are now poor, unemployment rates are high and until recently the language and culture had become all but forgotten. A movement to revive interest in and knowledge of the language and culture is associated with the creation of a new sense of self-respect and the strengthening of the Maori as a community.

Language nests for pre-school, and *kura* for primary school children were developed privately on a small scale during the 1980s. The recognition of the *kura* by the education system in 1989 thus represented support for efforts that had come out of the Maori community, rather than simply an affirmative action measure invented by government. By 1993, tentative steps were being taken to extend the concept of Maori education to the secondary and higher levels.

Examples of outcomes

- Kura Kaupapa Maori *have been established as a small but well-supported educational option.* The 1 384 pupils enrolled represent only a small proportion of the total Maori population. This is partly because the movement is still young, but also because the style of education and the commitment required do not appeal to all Maoris.
- *The level of parental commitment demanded varies considerably from one kura to another.* Some require active involvement of every parent in the running of the school, and specify that parents too must be committed to speaking the language. Others are more relaxed, and as a result appeal to a wider section of the community.
- *The attempt to develop Maori-language teaching at every level of education is significant,* as the objective of reviving a Maori-speaking community may fail if children only speak the language at primary school. But the fledgeling secondary school is finding it difficult to offer an adequate curriculum, given the complete lack of teaching materials and shortage of written texts in the Maori language.
- *An evaluation in 1992 of the extent to which* kura *were meeting their goals indicated good growth in the students' use of oral Maori,* in reading and in numeracy. There were also strong developments in personal confidence and a positive view towards Maori identity.

Commentary

This alternative choice within New Zealand education was created as a result of demand from its users rather than a government-designed initiative. However, that demand is not expressed in terms of choices in the market-place, but by the discussions of the users as a group: in the *kura* and in Maori culture generally, decisions are made by groups. There may be a danger in some cases that these groups, being self-defining, potentially exclude certain other families from benefiting from the *kura*, which may be defined too strictly for them. But it is in the nature of this initiative that it is run by groups with a strong sense of their mission, rather than by educational entrepreneurs trying to sell to a wide market. Perhaps a more fundamental risk is that the Maori movement as currently formulated will appear excessively separatist, and attract hostility from elsewhere in New Zealand society. Supporters of the movement, however, feel they have little to lose from attempting to re-establish a distinctive identity in a country in which their fortunes have languished over the past 150 years.

Case Study 11

Boston's universal form
of public enrolment choice *(United States)*

Like nine other cities in Massachusetts, Boston has abolished most links between residence and the assignment of public school places. All parents are required to list their school preferences, and places are distributed to satisfy as many choices as possible consistent with racial integration. Where choices conflict, residence only plays a small part in the distribution of places. "Parent information centres" help parents to make informed choices.

This system has produced some interesting results. The fact that 94 per cent of children in the school year 1993/94 were assigned to first- or second-choice schools, yet the majority did not opt for their nearest school, demonstrates an unusually even spread of preferences. The phenomenon of the best-informed parents flocking to a handful of socially favoured schools may have been avoided by forcing everyone to choose, spreading information as evenly as possible to all parents and making it virtually impossible for the most privileged to "play the system". An apparent increase in white participation in Boston public schools also indicates that fewer of the privileged are fleeing the system entirely.

Characteristics

- *"Controlled choice"* is used to make all school assignments to grade 1 (age 6), grade 6 (age 11) and grade 9 (age 14) in the Boston school district.
- *Parents are required to submit applications by a particular date,* listing in preference order at least two schools.
- *The school district authorities decide the number of places available at each school.* Students are assigned to these places in accordance with their choices, subject to the following priorities:
  - If any racial group is significantly over-represented at the school, in relation to the population of the "zone" where it is located, places for that group are "capped". (Boston is divided into three zones. A racial group may be over-represented by up to 10 per cent.)
  - Assignment priority is given first to children with siblings at the school, second to children moving to regular classes from bilingual and special education

classes, and third to students who choose only schools within walking distance of their homes.
- A special effort is made to maximise the number of people getting their first or second choice of school.
- The small proportion of children who do not get assigned to one of the schools that they have chosen get "mandatorily assigned" to a school with spare places.
– *To register for a place at an elementary school, all applicants must visit the parent information centre serving their zone.* These centres help parents to understand the application process, give them information on schools and offer various workshops and support for parents. Such services are significant in a city with many parents with low levels of education, and a high proportion whose native language is not English. The East Zone parent information centre, for example, offers bilingual assistance in nine languages.
– *Since the number of places at each school is preset, controlled choice does not give financial incentives to schools to attract more students.* Funding is not made proportional to enrolment levels. The least-chosen schools are targeted for improvement through the "STAR" programme, "Schools that are Restructuring". STAR schools get greater flexibility in spending, allowing them to pay for good staff development.

Background/evolution

Boston has been trying for a generation to make its public schools more racially balanced. Forced bussing in the early 1970s caused a storm of controversy and did not work, as privileged white parents could move beyond the district boundary or opt for private schools to avoid compulsory integration. The setting-up of a network of magnet schools, first introduced as early as 1969, provided a carrot rather than a stick for Whites to remain in a racially mixed system. This was effective in creating a group of desired and integrated schools. But failure to expand these schools with demand meant that places at popular schools became scarce. In 1984, a study carried out by Boston's Department of [Desegregation] Implementation found that one in three white students who failed to get their first choice of public elementary school was not in the city's schools a year later – compared to one in six white students who had got their first choice, one in ten black students who had not got their first choice and one in eight black students who had.

From this experience, it seemed evident that the only way to keep white families in the public school system, without allowing them to concentrate in a few élite schools, was to encourage them to choose among a wider range of options. The introduction of controlled choice challenged every public school to attract its students from around the city. A similar system had been introduced in Cambridge, Massachusetts, in 1981, with some encouraging results. Students of different races appeared to choose in similar ways, and the proportion of school-age children attending the city's public schools rose from 75 per cent in 1980 to 88 per cent in 1986. In 1989, Boston introduced "universal controlled choice", as did eight other Massachusetts cities at a similar time.

The rules under which this scheme operates have been changed as a result of early difficulties. Some of these have related to the nature of the applications procedure, which in its quest for fairness had been virtually incomprehensible to ordinary parents. A more fundamental change was the reduction in the use of random selection where preferences conflict. Originally, allocation to crowded schools had depended on the allocation of a random number to every pupil. Parents with a low number might have none of their preferences respected, and be assigned against their will to schools not in their neighbourhood. Even though such cases were relatively rare, the protests were loud, so the new system puts priority on meeting people's first and second choices, and on assigning a local school when that is desired.

Examples of outcomes

- In 1993, 96 per cent of pupils were assigned to one of the schools requested, 94 per cent to one of their first two choices and 85 per cent to their first choice.
- A minority of schools were significantly "over-chosen" or "under-chosen" by all racial groups, but a consultants' study[86] showed that these schools were not determined by neighbourhood.
- A majority (57 per cent) of pupils were assigned to schools to which they were transported by school bus. The concept of a "walk-to" school appears to appeal to only a minority of Boston parents. A contributing influence is the fact that walking in some parts of Boston is considered dangerous. Children who attend schools more than a prescribed distance from home are transported by a school bus from a street corner close to their homes. "When people are given a choice, they go for quality, not their neighbourhood school", says a school district official.
- The flight of Whites from Boston public schools appears at least to have been stemmed. The signs for the 1993/94 school year were that the proportion of white first-grade students could rise by 5-10 per cent.
- Parent information centres create a more accessible interface between parents and the school system than existed in the past. They strongly encourage parents to visit prospective schools. They also act as district offices to deal with such day-to-day matters as running the school bus system.
- Children, too, have become more actively involved in the choice of middle schools and high schools. Some children visit the information centres without their parents.
- In 1989, only seven parents put as their first choice the Lewis School, a middle school in a predominantly black area; only 31 put it anywhere on their list of choices, and 70 pupils were assigned there without having chosen it. A dynamic new principal and a restructuring programme as a STAR school had by 1993 reduced the number of forced assignments to 13. This failing school would probably have been rescued or closed regardless of the choice plan, but the principal points out an important difference: choice has forced her to "sell" the changes to the public. This has involved not only school fairs and other publicity, but also regular contacts with the community that have created active support for the school from parents and local businesses.

Commentary

Universal choice can only work well if parents' choices are spread fairly evenly across schools. Otherwise, a large proportion of preferences will not be met. Boston has had some success in this respect. The cause is hard to determine, but a number of factors could have helped. The weakening of neighbourhood as the prevailing criterion for school attendance might help loosen socially-generated school hierarchies. The universal nature of choice, with much emphasis on giving poorer people the means to make decisions based on the observation of schools, might have reduced the influence of "cocktail-party" gossip among the better-off in creating sought-after schools. The careful management of allocations according to consistent criteria by the school district might have made it harder for the more privileged to cluster by manipulating the system.

However, these promising signs should be put in the context of a public school system that has already lost most of its privileged customers. Only one-quarter of new enrolments in Boston public schools in 1993 were by Whites. Only if the universe of the city's public school clientele can itself expand will "universal choice" ultimately be judged a success.

Case Study 12

France's limited experiment in public enrolment choice[87]

Since the mid-1980s, there has been a relaxation (*assouplissement*) of rules allocating places at French public secondary schools. Formerly assigned to schools strictly according to residence, pupils in some parts of France are now able to apply to any lower or upper secondary school within a certain area. But choices outside one's home zone are permitted only if enrolment levels at each school stay between certain upper and lower limits. Higher enrolment is not matched by extra resources for a school.

Research on the experience of these new rules, in the case of lower secondary schools, shows that clear hierarchies have emerged among schools theoretically assumed to be equal. Official recognition of choice within the public sector tends to increase the educational advantages of certain social groups. But for less privileged groups that take advantage of this choice, most notably lower-middle-class families, it opens up new possibilities.

Characteristics

- The policy of *assouplissement* has been applied in selected geographical areas both to *collèges* (ages 11-15) since 1984 and to *lycées* (ages 15-18) since 1988. The following description applies to the case of the *collège*.
- The policy relaxes school-zoning regulations (*la sectorisation*) in specified geographical districts usually representing a *département* or a metropolitan area.
- A committee in each district fixes a higher and a lower limit on the number of pupils that can be admitted to the entry class in each school. Insofar as demand remains within those limits, families may enrol their children where they please. The committee is headed by an official of the Ministry of Education (the *Inspecteur d'Académie*), but includes representatives of local government and parents' associations.
- Applications made to a school outside one's "home" school zone may be rejected in one of two cases. First, if the higher limit of enrolments in the desired school would be exceeded. Second, if the lower limit of enrolments in the home school would not be met.
- In either of these cases, the committee selects who may leave or enter a school, according to the "acceptability" of reasons given by parents for wanting to transfer. A concrete reason such as the desire to study a rare language or to benefit

from a particular programme tends to be considered more acceptable than wanting a school with "a good reputation".
- Resources for schools are unaffected by the transfer of pupils outside their home school zone. The upper and lower enrolment levels represent limits to the class sizes considered acceptable in the context of a preset number of teachers for each school. Thus, the more popular a school, the larger the classes, within these limits.

Background/evolution

In 1963, in an effort to guarantee equal access to secondary education everywhere in the country, the French government drew up a *carte scolaire* (educational map) defining a precise catchment area for every *lycée* and *collège*. By the 1980s, however, this "sectorisation" had lost much of its legitimacy, as many families who did not like their local school were either enrolling in private schools (mainly subsidised Catholic schools) or finding pretexts for moving within the public sector. Pleas for dispensation for reasons such as a course only being taught at the school desired, as well as falsification of addresses, had apparently become commonplace. Parents with social and cultural advantages were best at manipulating the system.

In the early 1980s the Socialist Minister of Education, Alain Savary, attempted to subject private schools to greater public control, and to impose on them the same "sectorised" enrolment rules as public schools. The popular outrage arising from this proposal, which brought down a government, also demonstrated how powerful and widespread was the desire of French parents for a choice of school, even if only a minority exercised it. The relaxation of enrolment rules within the public sector, legislated on an experimental basis for *collèges* in 1983, was the first official recognition that choice within the public sector was a legitimate aspiration.

In 1984, the policy of *assouplissement* was introduced in five areas representing a small minority of *collèges*. In 1988, the policy was extended to certain *lycées*, including all the ones in Paris. By 1990, 47 per cent of *collèges* and 27 per cent of *lycées* were covered.

Examples of outcomes

A leading educational sociologist, Robert Ballion, was asked to assess the policy of *assouplissement* in *collèges* during 1984 and 1986. His findings, which give a detailed picture of the policy's outcomes,[88] include the following:
- For most parents, the right to choose schools is a freedom of recourse. An average of 11 per cent chose a *collège* outside their home zone. This number was no higher than average in urbanised *départements* with a number of attractive schools. It was no higher in the third year of *assouplissement* than in the year it was introduced. Of those who applied for a different school, three-quarters were accepted.
- However, the average does mask wide variations in the popularity of different schools. Ballion classifies the schools as follows, according to the difference between the number of out-of-zone pupils applying to enter and the number of

local pupils applying to leave (on average, there are 100 pupils in the entry year of each *collège*):
- *Highly-demanded*: a positive balance of more than 30 pupils, representing 10 per cent of schools. These are the only schools that attract pupils from a wide geographical area. Many were once attached to *lycées*, and some of these still benefit from shared resources. A high proportion of pupils are from professional and managerial families; a low proportion are manual workers or immigrants.
- *Demanded*: a positive balance of 10-29 pupils, representing 13 per cent of schools. These schools have fewer pretensions than the highly-demanded, and are often chosen by families with more modest social ambitions who do not expect to get a place at the highly-demanded. A common strength is that they are small and relatively more intimate than some of the large sites that include both a *lycée* and a *collège*.
- *Highly-rejected* and *rejected*: a negative balance equivalent to the demanded and highly-demanded categories. These represent 7 per cent and 17 per cent of schools respectively. Strangely, Ballion's study identified a larger number of less-desired characteristics in "rejected" than in "highly-rejected" schools – especially in terms of racial and social balance. Two possible explanations are that the highly-refused schools suffer from particular unidentified disadvantages (such as poor transport facilities) or that immigrants choose out-of-zone schools that offer languages such as Arabic or Portuguese. This underlines the point that not everybody chooses a school by the same criteria.
- *Balanced*: the 31 per cent of schools whose inflow roughly matches the outflow. These are frequently the more popular schools in working-class suburbs, that lose some pupils to schools in higher-class neighbourhoods but gain pupils from other working-class areas.
- *Flat*: the 21 per cent of schools with little movement in either direction. These are typically in rural areas where there are no realistic alternatives.

– Different social classes have very different propensities to choose outside their allocated school:

Families making a choice of *collège*, by socio-professional category

Category of head of household	As % of those making a choice of *collège* (%)	As % of total entrants to *collèges* (%)
Farmers	0.2	1.3
Craftsmen, shopkeepers, small businessmen	4.8	8.2
Managers, higher professionals	16.1	11.4
Intermediate professionals	17.4	18.5
Clerical workers	28.2	16.7
Manual workers	22.3	37.7
Teachers	11.0	6.2
Total	100.0	100.0

A survey[89] by the Ministry of Education carried out in 1991 found broadly similar results in the seventh year of operation of *assouplissement* – although the disparities between different groups was somewhat narrower. This survey also noted that variation by professional group was more noticeable when categorised by profession of working mother than by father, implying perhaps that women who work have a stronger influence on the school choice process than their husbands.

The families making the greatest number of choices compared to their share of the school population were those headed by a teacher. Taking both parents into account, some 20 per cent of active choosers had at least one teacher in the family. Higher professional and managerial classes were over-represented; manual workers under-represented. But the only broad socio-professional group as active in choosing as the teachers were the clerical workers. These lower-middle-class families are most likely to live in neighbourhoods shared with manual workers, in a milieu that they fear might compromise the aspiration of upward mobility that they project on their children.

One other distinctive feature of "choosers" was a high level of "activism" in relation to schools. Nearly 40 per cent belonged to parents' associations, twice the average, and a high proportion of these had positions of responsibility in the associations. This phenomenon is similar to that observed among parents using vouchers to escape public schools in Milwaukee, the United States (see Case Study 15).

- Of the reasons officially given by parents for wanting to choose an out-of-zone school, the great majority (66 per cent) were "domestic". Such reasons included transport considerations, a sibling at the school or a hypothetical intention of moving to the area. Only 27 per cent cited reasons related to the school's quality, character or reputation. However, this may show mainly that parents know how to "play the system": domestic reasons are more likely to be given priority. When asked for a list of motives by researchers, nearly half the parents cited at least one reason linked to the school's reputation.
- The overall result of greater choice is to accentuate differences between *collèges* catering for different populations. This is most evident at the two poles: on the one hand, privileged schools preparing an élite for an academically-oriented *lycée*; on the other, schools in poor neighbourhoods that specialise in helping children "in difficulty" or offering mother-tongue tuition to immigrants. Ballion suggests that this represents a return towards a situation that existed before the creation of a single form of lower secondary school.[90]

Commentary

The French case illustrates how even limited school choice can undermine certain official objectives of an education system, yet result from pressures that are inescapable. The attempt to create a common and equal *collège* had already been undermined by "back-door" choice in the public sector and choice of private schools, even before public sector choice became official. While the new policy may accentuate the trend towards socially segregated schools, it appears on balance to have created more equal access for individuals to better-regarded schools. In particular, it has permitted more choosing among lower-middle-class families who had not had the connections to "play the system" when it officially assigned everybody to the local school.

Case Study 13

Minnesota: public-sector challenges to school district monopolies *(United States)*

Since the mid-1980s, a series of measures passed by the state legislature have given Minnesota parents certain alternatives to sending their children to schools run by their local school district. The three main ones have been: *inter-district enrolment* – the possibility of transferring to a school in another district; *post-secondary enrolment* – the possibility of completing high school at a post-secondary institution; and *charter schools* – the creation of public schools with new educational ideas, outside local district control. Although these initiatives were not conceived as a single plan, they all aim to create incentives for school improvement by preventing districts from taking their student population for granted. While the numbers so far exercising choice have been modest, it is widely believed that the possibility of choice has made some local authorities more responsive.

Characteristics

- *Inter-district enrolment* allows students to attend elementary and secondary schools outside their home district. This is subject to available space in the accepting district, but cannot be blocked by the district of residence. For each student who transfers, the state reduces subsidy to the sending district and increases subsidy to the receiving one by an amount equal to average per-pupil expenditure. Since the marginal cost per pupil is generally lower than the average, there is a financial incentive for districts to retain students living within their boundaries, and to attract those living elsewhere.
- *Post-secondary enrolment* options provide 11th- and 12th-grade students (ages 16-18) the opportunity to take college courses for high school credit. This may give students access to a wider variety of courses, and also to obtain college credits before graduating from high school. Any degree-granting post-secondary institution, offering general or vocational courses, may participate.
- *Charter schools* are independent public schools set up by educators with innovative ideas. Operating outside the jurisdiction of the school district, and exempt from much of the regulation governing district-run schools, charter schools are funded directly by the state government. Each is governed by a teacher-dominated board. Limitations on the creation of charter schools in the initial state legislation

included the requirement of the support of a school board (though not necessarily the local one) before the charter could be granted, and the restriction of the number of such schools to two per district and eight (later raised to 20) in the state.

Background/evolution

In the mid-1980s, Governor Rudy Perpich made choice within the public sector central to school reform in Minnesota, after being persuaded that persistent attempts to improve public schools had yielded patchy or temporary results. The introduction of some competition for districts was intended to create a fixed incentive for sustained improvement. Minnesota was the first American state to pursue explicitly the idea of choice within the public sector; previously, choice had generally been interpreted as meaning public support for private schools.

Post-secondary enrolment options were introduced in 1985, inter-district enrolment in 1987 and the first charter school opened in 1992.

Examples of outcomes

Each of these three options has affected only a small minority of Minnesota pupils. In 1991/92, 9 885 out of 750 000 Minnesota schoolchildren were enrolled outside their home district; 7 534 out of 102 000 11th- to 12th-graders were enrolled in post-secondary courses – though both these figures were steadily growing. The eight charter schools approved by early 1993 included: a Montessori school, a school for the deaf, schools involving students in designing their own learning and a school for at-risk children.

Despite the low numbers participating, there is some evidence (not systematically assessed) of impact on district behaviour. Inter-district enrolment has caused at least one relatively disadvantaged suburb to work harder to raise money and attract parents. The Westonka school district, which is surrounded by districts with good reputations, introduced a "technology plan" for all its public schools to offer an identifiable advantage. In the first year of open enrolment, the superintendent interviewed every one of the families applying for school places outside the district. In the event, only half of those applying to leave actually did so.

Post-secondary enrolment appears to have encouraged more schools to offer more advanced (college-level) courses, although some would have done so anyway. One district presented with an application for a Montessori charter school decided to establish one itself instead.

There have been scattered examples of cross-district movements causing perverse or undesirable effects, but even critics acknowledge that there have not been major disadvantages, and that the small overall numbers precluded serious financial losses to disadvantaged districts. The complaint getting the most publicity in the spring of 1993 was the tendency (more perceived than actual) of students to move to schools strong in hockey, a sport with which Minnesotans are obsessed.

Commentary

Public sector choices in Minnesota appear to have generated a certain amount of dynamism within a school system which, while generally considered to be good by parents and the public, risked being complacent. However, the relatively low level of controversy has undoubtedly been linked partly to the measures' relatively modest impact. Charter schools, the latest innovation, create more fierce debate, and have on the whole been opposed by vested interests such as school superintendents and teacher unions. If this experiment is extended to the point that it starts encroaching significantly on school district enrolments, debate could become more fierce. One significant initial characteristic has been the tendency of charter schools to look for "niche" markets rather than trying to compete with districts to provide a standard education. The effect of this is both to increase the amount of qualitative choice available to parents and to reduce direct conflict between charter and district schools, whose roles may be complementary.

Case Study 14

Denmark's "free" schools – liberal support for private education

Denmark's private schools receive about 80 per cent of their costs from the national government. They are known as "free schools" – an apt description, given the liberal attitude of government to this sector, compared to other governments that subsidise private education. As long as parents show commitment to a school, and the basic subjects are taught, it can do more or less as it pleases. A diverse range of free schools have emerged as a result since the first one opened in 1852. This sector has grown recently to 11 per cent of compulsory school enrolments.

In 1991 the financing of free schools was changed to a system more closely linked to pupil enrolments. Small schools get more per pupil than large ones, in proportions recommended by the free school organisation. Capital grants are also linked automatically to pupil numbers. In this way the government is able to take political decisions about the overall funding of schools while allowing the structure of provision to be determined entirely by the choices of schools and parents.

Characteristics

- Free schools provide education for all or part of the school years, ages 6 to 18.
- Each free school must be governed by a board elected by parents. The parents are responsible for appointing an inspector if standards are considered unsatisfactory. To ensure that parents have a stake in the school, the government specifies that fees must be at least DKr 3 500 a year; although this may be reduced on the grounds of need. Other than these measures to ensure parent involvement, the government does not interfere with the running of free schools, although they are required in principle to give education on the same level as public schools.
- Each school receives a subsidy for each pupil equal to a percentage of the per-pupil cost of running public schools. On average, this percentage was 72 in 1993. Since free schools were assumed to spend 10 per cent less per pupil than public schools, due to savings on items such as teaching pupils with special needs, they were expected to raise on average 20 per cent of their costs from fees. But the actual subsidy varies according to school size. The smallest schools get subsidy at 1.45 times the largest schools. The government decides the average rate

(72 per cent) but the small-large variation is negotiated among the free schools themselves within their association, before being enacted by the parliament.
- Schools also receive a capital element in their per-pupil subsidy. Since capital costs vary, this may often be considerably more or significantly less than a school needs for capital, but it avoids the need for a complex formula or direct government involvement in planning free school provision.
- Free schools are typically smaller than public schools ("folk schools"). Over 40 per cent of free schools, containing 15 per cent of their pupils, enrol fewer than 100. Only 15 per cent of folk schools, with 3 per cent of their pupils, do so.
- Free schools have many different identities, with no one dominant. They include independent rural schools, academically-oriented lower secondary schools, some religious schools, progressive free schools, Rudolf Steiner schools, German minority schools and immigrant schools such as Muslim schools.

Background/evolution

Free schools originally grew out of the Grundtvigian movement, which in the 19th century led to the establishment of liberal schools for farming communities that rejected formal education systems and wanted school to be related directly to life. Another long-established strand provides academically-oriented schools serving well-to-do families with high aspirations for their children. In the 1960s, various "progressive" schools were set up in cities by parents espousing radical ideas. Free schools grew in popularity during the 1980s, rising from 8 per cent of enrolments in 1982/83 to 11 per cent in 1991/92.

The change in the funding system in 1991 was a means of controlling costs more efficiently while leaving allocation in the hands of the schools themselves. This was a masterly political move. Under a more complex formula, small schools had been getting a progressively higher level of per-capita funding to support their high average costs. This upset the municipalities, who found that when they closed small schools that were too costly, they would open again as private ones; municipalities must reimburse to central government most of the subsidy paid to free schools within their boundaries. The system also upset larger free schools, who felt that they were getting a progressively smaller share of the subsidy. Under the new system, subsidies are related more directly to pupil numbers, with the level of weighting to small schools transparent. The government is able to set the overall level of subsidy according to political priorities, and let the free schools decide the rest.

Examples of outcomes

- The *laissez-faire* approach to private schools in Denmark produces a diversity unparalleled in other OECD countries. Elsewhere, where over 10 per cent of children enrol in private schools, big religious sectors tend to dominate.
- Parent control makes free schools sensitive to parental views, in various ways. These can include decision-making by the board, the power of exit, and direct involvement of individual parents in school activities. All three are illustrated by the following example:

- *Albertslund Lilleskole* was established in 1968 in a large old house in a suburb of Copenhagen. It was one of a group of *lilleskoler* or "little schools" set up with a socialist philosophy and a "free" pedagogy similar to England's Summerhill. By the late 1980s, the school was losing pupils, had chaotic management and local rumour was that its pupils had difficulty reading and writing. Decisions had hitherto been taken by committees of ideologically-committed parents. A new principal saved the school from demise by taking charge of its management, underplaying the socialism and strengthening the teaching of basic skills, while retaining a "progressive" philosophy and a curriculum stressing creative subjects. The school's rolls rose from 60 to 150. The school now emphasizes direct involvement of parents in the classroom, where they co-operate with the school in reaching its goals. Previously, their involvement had been on endlessly conflictual committees. The principal believes that the fall in enrolments that eventually caused the school to alter represented a change in the demands coming from parents. Even liberal-minded ones want their children to acquire the basic skills and disciplines needed in late 20th century society, the principal observes.
- The stress on parental governance prevents managed networks of schools from being set up. Even though schools like *lilleskoler* follow a common philosophy, each one is self-managed and distinctive. This limits the degree to which provision will respond to demand through duplication or expansion, especially with schools that would not want to become too large. New schools only start up when demand takes the form of group commitment within a local community.
- In theory, support for free schools is justified partly by the idea that municipal schools will benefit from their experience. In practice, there is little replication of pedagogical practices from one sector to another. But municipal schools are starting to replicate the model of parental involvement developed in free schools. In 1989, school boards with a majority of parent members were established at all folk schools, and increasing decentralisation to these boards is foreseen. Parents are also gradually obtaining a freer choice of folk school within their municipality.

Commentary

Denmark is willing to provide a wide degree of choice through private schools on the sole condition that parents are in control of the school. In some cases, this presents risks that would not be acceptable in every country. There has been some concern about dubious organisations operating bogus schools. There is a degree of "creaming-off" of middle-class children which contributes to the creation of "ghetto" public schools in central Copenhagen. There is a risk of children whose parents have extreme ideas failing to get what many would consider an adequate education. All of these risks are accepted because they do not create huge problems in a stable, tolerant and relatively homogeneous country, more at ease with itself than some others. Transplanted to the United States, the Danish system would in all likelihood have supported with public money a Branch Davidian school in Waco, Texas, with David Koresh writing the curriculum. But since Denmark is not the United States, the system works to the satisfaction of most Danes.

Case Study 15

Milwaukee's vouchers – limited support for private education *(United States)*

Milwaukee, Wisconsin, is the only place in the United States where public money finances tuition for children attending private schools. The state government's subsidy for public schools may be used instead as a tuition fee for poor pupils enrolling in non-religious private schools. Although limited in its scope and restricted in its size, this scheme illustrates how some poor families welcome the choice of private education. But it avoids a central issue in the American debate over "vouchers": the impact on public schools of a rush to private education.

Characteristics

- Under the Milwaukee Parental Choice Program, a transfer of public funds is made to private schools for each eligible pupil enrolled, in lieu of their tuition. The grant is equal to the per-pupil grant of the state to the school district, about $2 700 in 1992/93.
- To be eligible, the pupil's family must have an income not exceeding 1.75 times the national poverty line. The pupil may not have attended another private school or a school outside Milwaukee in the year before enrolling.
- Participating schools may not have a religious affiliation, may not receive the subsidy for more than 49 per cent of their pupils and must use random selection to admit pupils if their rolls are over-subscribed.
- In total, the number of pupils benefiting from this scheme may not exceed 1 per cent of the total number of pupils enrolled in Milwaukee's public schools.
- By the third year of operation, 1992/93, 11 schools and 613 pupils were participating.

Background/evolution

Milwaukee is a city with heavy levels of deprivation, a high rate of student turnover in its schools and a drop-out rate estimated at 40 per cent. Some children are bussed from the city to suburbs under a state-sponsored integration plan; others are bussed around the city.

In the late 1980s, the idea of vouchers for private schools was taken up by a group of black legislators and community leaders led by a charismatic state representative, Polly Williams. They resented the idea that the only way for black inner-city children to get a good education was to be bussed miles out of town. They saw local, private schools as the only possible alternative to the public schools that they believed were failing their children.

The scheme was passed through the Wisconsin state legislature in 1990, against the opposition of the state superintendent of schools but with the support of the state governor. The restrictions put on the scheme, most notably the exclusion of religious schools, were designed to make it acceptable to legislators and the courts. Its legality was upheld by four votes to three in the Wisconsin Supreme Court in March 1992.

Examples of outcomes[91]

- The scheme has grown slowly, with just under half of private non-sectarian schools participating by 1992/93.
- Families who participated had incomes on average well below the stipulated maximum. Three-quarters were Blacks and 20 per cent were Hispanics. More (76 per cent) were in families with single parents than on average in low-income families attending Milwaukee public schools (64 per cent).
- Over half (52 per cent) of mothers in participating families had college education, compared with 40 per cent in Milwaukee public schools and 30 per cent in low-income families in the public schools.
- As well as being better educated than the average, families that chose privately had been more active in the public school system. For example, 60 per cent had taken part in parent-teacher organisation activities, compared to 35 per cent on average. These were typically parents who had been the most vocal in demanding improvements in their public schools, and who had been most directly involved in the education of their children.
- Parents typically chose private schools because they were unhappy with how much their children were learning and with school discipline. There was no clear trend of improvement in measured pupil performance after transfer to the private schools, although a small sample and a high attrition rate has made this hard to assess. However, parent satisfaction with schools showed a clear improvement in every category.
- The schools involved were varied in character and quality. Typical attributes were high parental involvement, attention to ethnic issues and instability due largely to high teacher turnover related to low pay. In some cases, the voucher scheme has created greater financial stability. Of five new schools joining the scheme in 1992, three were Montessori and one a Waldorf school.

Commentary

Choice has undoubtedly improved the overall educational satisfaction of the small number of families who left the Milwaukee public school system to receive private education free of charge. It has helped to support genuine educational alternatives. It appears not to have had a significant impact on the public system, because the number of children involved has been so low. However, the profile of participating families indicates that a larger scheme might have a significant detrimental impact on public schools. Even in a voucher scheme restricted to the poor, there is a noticeable difference between the characteristics of parents who choose private schools and those remaining with public ones: the choosers are better educated and more active in the school system. Their loss, in numbers greater than the Milwaukee scheme permits, could potentially make public education even more of a ghetto.

Case Study 16

New Zealand's educational development initiatives: community-wide choice
Two examples

Educational development initiatives (EDIs) were created in New Zealand as a method of developing local educational change through community consultation, in a framework requiring central government approval. Change may involve the development of new educational ideas, but is centred on the structure of school provision, and in particular the division of responsibility for primary, intermediate and secondary schooling among various schools in an area. This type of initiative can partly be seen as a new method of system-wide school planning and rationalisation following the liberalising of enrolment rules and the devolving of school management. For that reason, there has been a certain amount of scepticism about the degree to which it is likely to lead to qualitative improvement in education.

The following examples illustrate how EDIs have developed in two New Zealand towns. Both were still in progress in 1993. In each case, community-wide collaboration through EDIs has been seen as a desirable alternative to inter-school competition initially created by open enrolment and school autonomy.

Levin EDI

Characteristics

The two secondary schools (ages 13-18) in this small town near Wellington are developing a proposal to merge into a single college, with an upper and lower school on separate sites. This new institution would include some tertiary and adult education courses, and might also involve some degree of merger with the intermediate school (ages 11-13). As well as using economies of scale to offer a wide range of courses, the new institution would attempt to develop a new style of pupil-centred learning.

Background/evolution

In 1987 a varied group of people from the community came together to discuss how to improve secondary schooling in a town where it was felt that a number of pupils were failing to acquire some basic educational skills. They met over several years and developed a broad framework for improving education. Eventually a more concrete model was drawn up by a group dominated by the school principals in the area. By 1993, there were plans to submit this for wide consultation – initially to staff and community representatives for refinement, then to parents and boards of trustees and eventually to the Education Minister for approval. This rather lengthy process formally became an educational development initiative in 1991.

Examples of outcomes

It is envisaged that the plan will be implemented in 1995.

Commentary

The idea of merging the two schools has strong educational motives. However, there are also two important influences related to competition among schools. One is the competition, now common in New Zealand, among various kinds of school for students of "intermediate" age (11-13). The intermediate school in Levin is already competing with rural primary schools in the area, that accept children up to the age of 13. One of the urban primaries has also applied to extend itself to include 11-13 year-olds. One way for the intermediate school to protect its enrolment is to co-operate with the high schools to create a package of 11-18 year-old education in which the intermediate would provide a useful introduction to the secondary programme. The second influence is competition between the two high schools, each of which wants to preserve and enhance its student base under the recently-introduced open enrolment rules. In a small town, such competition is considered unseemly and counter-productive, and any means of avoiding it is widely welcomed.

The length of this consultation process illustrates how difficult it can be to develop a local consensus around educational change, and to win the confidence of a community around plans that are inevitably formulated by educational professionals.

Whangarei EDI

Characteristics

Wide community consultation was in 1993 suggesting ways in which to organise schooling in this city. The Ministry of Education was considering these proposals as a package rather than looking individually at various applications by schools to change their intake. The consultation produced a variety of suggestions for better serving various educational needs in Whangarei.

Background/evolution

When a secondary school in Whangarei acted to meet a "market" demand, it set off a chain reaction that threatened to create dissension and bitterness in this small city north of Auckland. The central cause was that one of the high schools, Tikipunga, had its enrolment level threatened by the fact that there was no intermediate school situated geographically to act as a natural "feeder" to this high school. With the encouragement of the parents of its pupils, Tikipunga therefore successfully applied to the government to create an attached intermediate section. Simultaneously, a primary school successfully applied to "recapitate" (to admit 11 and 12 year-olds), and others applied to follow suit. The result was a squeeze on intermediate schools, one of which lost 60 enrolments almost overnight. In short, the schools in Whangarei were jockeying for competitive advantage, with the government acting as a referee by saying who was allowed to admit which kinds of pupil.

An alternative proposed by the Ministry of Education was to ask the community whether it would prefer to resolve these matters through consultation. It received a positive response, and set up a planning committee, carefully chosen among local people in a manner designed to rise above vested interests while bringing together a range of personal skills. Thus an EDI was established in 1992. These efforts from the central government were not the only attempt at collaboration rather than competition: a boys' and a girls' high school together with an intermediate school had already set up a joint council. Its aim was to combine protection of the intermediate school market with particular educational innovations designed to appeal to parents.

Examples of outcomes

The planning group drew up a range of options which were being considered in 1993. A final set of proposals would be subject to ministerial approval. The proposals included:
- retention of the current structure of schools in Whangarei;
- various proposals for changes in school organisation, including an innovative proposal for a new style of four-year junior high school not yet tried in New Zealand, or alternatively the transformation of Tikipunga into a forms 1-7 (intermediate plus high) school;
- the establishment of a "Kura Kaupapa Maori" school in Whangarei (see Case Study 10), for which a good case had been made;
- measures to support the effective integration of children with special needs into mainstream schooling.

Commentary

It seemed likely by mid-1993 that this consultation process would mainly confirm the right of schools to make the structural changes that they had already proposed. The unlikelihood of adopting some of the radical ideas reflects a certain conservatism built into the process, since proposals that might offend a certain section of the community tend to be ruled out. However, the consultation in itself played a critical legitimating function. The creation of an EDI was welcomed as an alternative to an unseemly rush by schools to "carve up the pupil market". In a small town, few people had welcomed the atmosphere created by this kind of competition. An important spin-off effect of the consultation was to reveal demand for things that had not been provided in the past – addressing in particular the case for better serving the Maori population and children with special needs. These are demands that do not necessarily emerge through individual schools' competition to meet demand. Educational development initiatives thus serve to some extent to replace local educational planning, but hand the initiative from bureaucrats to communities.

Notes

1. The papers are available from the ODCE/CERI Secretariat, 2, rue André-Pascal, 75775 Paris Cedex 16, France. This series, "School Choice: Background report to CERI", comprises:
   Australia (Commonwealth government), *by the Department of Employment, Education and Training.*
   Australia (New South-Wales) *by Lesley Lynch.*England, *by Dick Booth.*
   Netherlands, *by Jaap Dronkers.*
   New Zealand, *by Eddie Clark.*
   Sweden, *by Annika Andrea Thelin.*
   United States, *by Charles Glenn.*
2. England rather than the United Kingdom is the subject of the specific country study in this report. However, when reference is made in the general text to policies of the British government, other parts of the United Kingdom are implicitly included.
3. J.S. Mill (1859), *On Liberty,* Parker, London.
4. These points are expanded in OECD/CERI, "The lifelong learner in the 1990s" and in A. Tuijnman and M. van der Kamp, eds. (1992), *Learning Across the Lifespan: Theories, Research, Policies,* Chaptersn 1-2, 13-15, Oxford: Pergamon Press.
5. M. Friedman (1962), *Capitalism and Freedom,* University of Chicago Press, Chicago.
6. J.E. Chubb and T.M. Moe (1990), *Politics, Markets and America's Schools,* Brookings Institution, Washington, D.C.
7. R. Ballion (1991), *La bonne école,* Hatier, Paris, p. 18.
8. An interesting manifestation of this was the enormous popularity of academically selective schools when they were reintroduced in New South Wales, despite the fact that they were arbitrarily-chosen former comprehensive schools that had undergone no signficant change in their teaching staff, structure or curriculum. See Case Study 6 below.
9. See section on "Examples of impact" in New Zealand summary (Part II).
10. See Chapter 3, section on "Choice and programme diversity".
11. Department of Education (1992), *Choice and Diversity, A New Framework for Schools,* HMSO, London, Chapter 10.
12. P.A. Woods (1993), "Parental perspectives on choice in the United Kingdom: Preliminary thoughts on meanings and realities of choice in education". Annual Meeting of the American Educational Research Association, Atlanta, April. R. Glatter and P.A. Woods (1993), "Competitive arenas in education: Studying the impact of enhanced competition and choice on parents and schools". Conference on "Quasi-Markets: The emerging findings", University of Bristol.
13. S. Ball, R. Bowe and S. Gewirtz (1992), "Circuits of schooling: A sociological exploration of parental choice of school in social class contexts", Economic and Social Research Council, Swindon, United Kingdom.

14. Surveys reported in R. Ballion (1989), *Le choix du lycée,* Ministère de l'Éducation nationale, Paris, Convention N° 88-89, pp. 24-25.
15. R. Ballion (1982), *Les consommateurs d'école,* Stock, Paris, p. 194.
16. Temo Testhuset Marknad Opinion (1993), *Det Fria Skolvalet – en attitydundersökning bland föräldrar till barn i grundsolan för Skolverket, januari 1993,* Temo, Solna, Sweden.
17. This work – by M. Adler, A. Petch and J. Tweedie – and other Scottish studies by Macbeth, Strachan and Macaulay and by Echols, McPherson and Willms are summarised by Geoffrey Walford (1992), "Educational choice and equity in Great Britain", *Education Policy,* June, pp. 126-128.
18. P.G. Carpenter and J.S. Western (1992), "Choosing non-government secondary schooling", *Australian Educational Researcher,* pp. 23-37.
19. R. Ballion (1989), *op. cit.,* p. 30.
20. R. Ballion (1991), *op. cit.*
21. See Case Study 12.
22. See M. Adler, A. Petch and J. Tweedie (1989), *Parental Choice and Educational Policy,* Edinburgh University Press, Edinburgh.
23. S. Ball, R. Bowe and S. Gewirtz (1992), *op. cit.*
24. *Ibid.,* p. 5.
25. P.A. Woods (1993), *op. cit.,* p. 4.
26. G. Whitty, T. Edwards and S. Gewirtz (1993), *Specialisation and Choice in Urban Education: The city technology college experiment,* Routledge, London, pp. 83-84.
27. For example, the work on London being carried out at King's College, and Robert Ballion's work in Paris, both cited above.
28. In principle, judgements of schools' effectiveness should be based on their ability to produce a desired level of educational quality. In practice, the notion of quality and the notion of effectiveness have been addressed in relation to different versions of education's objectives. In particular, studies of "effectiveness" have tended to judge schools against easily quantifiable measures of pupil performance rather than a rounded assessment of educational quality. Thus, the possibility of links between choice and measurable effectiveness, discussed below, tells only part of the story. A link between choice and school quality more widely would be even harder to demonstrate. The notion of school quality is discussed in OECD (1989), *Schools and Quality*: An International Report, OECD, Paris.
29. J.S. Coleman, T. Hoffer and S. Kilgore (1982), *High School Achievement: Public, Catholic and Private Schools Compared,* Basic Books, New York.
30. H. Schijf and J. Dronkers (1993), "Are denominational primary schools a better choice?", Department of Statistics and Methodology, University of Amsterdam.
31. HMI (1993), *Grant Maintained Schools 1989-90 – A Report from the Office of Her Majesty's Chief Inspector of Schools,* HMSO, London.
32. J.S. Coleman and T. Hoffer (1987), *Public and Private High Schools: The Impact of Communities,* Basic Books, New York.
33. Schijf and Dronkers, *op. cit.* See also Dronkers (1993), "The existence of parental choice in the Netherlands", November.
34. See Swedish summary in Part II.
35. A distinction first made by A. Hirschman (1970), *Exit, Voice and Loyalty,* Harvard University Press, Cambridge.
36. J. Dronkers (1993), "The existence of parental choice in the Netherlands", *op. cit.*

37. More details on East Harlem can be found, for example, in R.F. Elmore (1991), "Community School District 4, New York City: A case of choice". Center for Policy Research in Education, Rutgers University, New York, and R.F. Elmore (1992), *School Choice,* The Carnegie Foundation for the Advancement of Teaching Foundation, Princeton, New Jersey, Chapter 3.
38. See, for example, in the Summary on England, "Choice patterns in practice".
39. In the six countries in this study, the number of 5-9 year-olds will rise by between 6 per cent (in the United Kingdom) and 31 per cent (in Sweden) from 1990 to 2005. For 10-14 year-olds, the rise will be between 13 per cent (New Zealand) and 22 per cent (Sweden, the United States): OECD (1993), *Education in OECD Countries 1988/89-1989/90,* p. 121, Table 7.1.
40. T. Bush *et al.* (1993), *Managing Autonomous Schools,* Paul Chapman, London.
41. This model is supported, for example, by the Scottish research cited in Chapter 2.
42. See Coleman *et al.* (1992), *op. cit.*
43. See, for example, John E. Coons and Stephen D. Sugerman (1992), *Scholarships for Children,* Institute of Governmental Studies Press, Berkeley.
44. OECD (1987), *Multicultural Education,* OECD, Paris, p. 340.
45. See Case Study 1, and the section on "Choice and programme diversity" in Chapter 3.
46. J.E. Chubb and T.M. Moe (1990), *Politics, Markets and America's Schools,* Brookings Institution, Washington, D.C.
47. P.G. Carpenter and J.S. Western (1992), "Choosing non-government secondary schooling", *Australian Educational Researcher,* pp. 23-37.
48. T. Williams and P.G. Carpenter (1990), "Private schooling and public achievement", *Australian Journal of Education,* pp. 3-34.

    D.S. Anderson (1992), "Long-term effects of public and private schooling", XIIth World Congress of Sociology, Madrid, July.
49. P.G. Carpenter and J.S. Western (1992), *op. cit.*
50. D. Anderson (1992), "The interaction of public and private school systems", *Australian Journal of Education,* pp. 213-236.
51. Although the British government's educational policies follow broadly similar principles in England, Scotland and Wales, many details vary. This section looks specifically at the case of England.
52. This evidence is outlined in Dick Booth's background report on England prepared for this study, available from OECD/CERI.
53. P.A. Woods (forthcoming), "Choice, class and effectiveness", *School Effectiveness and School Improvement.*
54. S. Ball, R. Bowe and S. Gewirtz (1992), *op. cit.*
55. HMI (1993), *Grant Maintained Schools 1989-90 – A Report from the Office of Her Majesty's Chief Inspector of Schools,* HMSO, London.
56. Association of Metropolitan Authorities (1993), *Choice of School, A Survey 1992-93,* London, p. 13.
57. See Chapter 2 above for further discussion.
58. J. Dronkers (1993), *op. cit.*
59. OECD (1991), *Reviews of National Policies for Education: Netherlands,* OECD, Paris, p. 75.
60. The minimum size rules, which are rather complex, were revised for secondary schools in 1992; proposals before Parliament for primary schools at the time of writing were scheduled for introduction in 1994. With secondary schools, the basic minimum of 30 pupils per year-group was supplemented by a basic minimum of 240 per school; in each case the minimum

may be higher if the school has more than one section. For primary schools, minimum sizes ranging from 50 to 125 according to size of municipality are being replaced by a range from 23 to 200 according to density of pupils in the municipality. But in both cases a primary school that falls below the minimum may be allowed to stay open if it is the last school in the area of a particular denomination.

61. J.F.A. Braster (1993), "Pluralism in education and society: The Dutch case", International Symposium on Law and Education, Max Planck Institute for Human Development and Education, Berlin, March 24-26, p. 10.
62. J. Dronkers (1993), *op. cit.*
63. G.M. Eadie (1993), "Parental choice of secondary school in the Hutt Valley", Master of Education degree thesis, Victoria University of Wellington.
64. The Heylen Research Centre, in their 1991 "A survey of public opinion on aspects of the current education system", found that 54 per cent of respondents believed private schools were "better", and 48 per cent were in favour of government paying fees to private schools up to 100 per cent of the cost of State school attendance, with 30 per cent opposed.
65. Education Act 1992, Chapter 9.
66. *Ibid.*
67. Temo Testhuset Marknad Opinion, *op. cit.*
68. Ingrid Jonsson and Goran Arnman (1989), "Social segregation in Swedish comprehensive schools", in Stephen J. Ball and Staffan Larsson (eds.), *The Struggle for Democratic Education – Equality and participation in Sweden,* The Falmer Press, Lewes, England.
69. C. Glenn (1993), "Parent choice of schools in the United States", OECD/CERI report prepared for the project, November.
70. See Case Study 11. Also Glenn *et al.* (1993), *Parent Information for School Choice: The case of Massachusetts,* Center on Families, Communities, Schools and Children's Learning, Boston.
71. J. Chubb and T. Moe (1990), *Politics, Markets and America's Schools,* Brookings Institution, Washington.

    See section on "History and politics" below.
72. M. Friedman (1962), *Capitalism and Freedom,* University of Chicago Press, Chicago.
73. J.S. Coleman, T. Hoffer and S. Kilgore (1982), *op. cit.*

    J.S. Coleman and T. Hoffer (1987), *op. cit.*
74. U.S. Commission on Excellence in Education (1983), *A Nation at Risk,* Government Printing Office, Washington, D.C.
75. J.E. Chubb and T.M. Moe (1990), *op. cit.*
76. Gallup surveys show that in 1991, 50 per cent of the public favoured vouchers available equally to public and private schools.
77. For example, M. Metz (1986), *Different by Design,* Routledge and Kegan Paul, New York. See also C. Rossell (1985), "What is attractive about magnet schools", *Urban Education,* April.
78. L. Darling-Hammond and S. Kirby (1987), "Public policy and private choice: The case of Minnesota", in T. James and H. Levin, eds. (1988), *Comparing Public and Private Schools, Volume 1: Institutions and Organisations,* Falmer Press, New York, pp. 247-8.
79. Coleman *et al.* (1982), *op. cit.* Raywid (1989), *The Case for Public Schools of Choice,* Phi Delta Kappan Educational Foundation, Bloomington, Indiana.
80. D.R. Moore *et al.* (1990), "School choice: The new improved sorting machine?", in W.L. Boyd and H.J. Walberg (eds.), *Choice in Education: Potential and Problems,* McCutchan, Berkeley.

81. R.K. Blank *et al.* (1983), *Survey of Magnet Schools: Analyzing a Model for Quality Integrated Education,* James Lowry Associates, Chicago. C.H. Rossell (1990), *The Carrot or the Stick for School Desegregation Policy,* Temple University Press, Philadelphia.
82. Research into the first 100 grant-maintained schools carried out at Leicester University found, for example, that 30 per cent of the "comprehensive" schools were subjectively using school reports, parental or pupil interviews or examinations to help select pupils. T. Bush *et al.* (1993), *Managing Autonomous Schools,* Paul Chapman, London.
83. This case study draws substantially from the most detailed analysis of city technology colleges during their early years: G. Whitty, T. Edwards and S. Gewirtz (1993), *Specialisation and Choice in Urban Education,* Routledge, London.
84. Whitty *et al., ibid.,* pp. 82-90.
85. Barbara Strobert (1991), "Factors influencing parental choice in selection of a magnet school in the Montclair, New Jersey, public schools", doctorate dissertation, Columbia Teachers College.
86. C.V. Willie and M.J. Alves (1993), "A report on the implementation of the revised Boston 'Controlled choice' plan", unpublished paper, Boston, March.
87. This case study draws much of its information from R. Ballion (1991), *La bonne école, op. cit.,* note 7.
88. *Ibid.,* pp. 178-199.
89. *L'autonomie de l'établissement,* ministère de l'Éducation nationale, Direction de l'évaluation et de la prospective, CREDOC, Paris, 1993.
90. R. Ballion (1991), *La bonne école, op. cit.,* p. 197.
91. This section is based on the assessment of the Milwaukee scheme commissioned by Wisconsin's Department for Public Instruction: J.F. Witte, A.B. Bailey and C.A. Thorn (1992), "Second year report". Milwaukee Parental Choice Program, Department of Political Science, University of Wisconsin-Madison, December. Except where otherwise stated, figures are for 1991/92.

Ministry of Education & Training
MET Library
13th Floor, Mowat Block, Queen's Park
Toronto   M7A 1L2

MAIN SALES OUTLETS OF OECD PUBLICATIONS
PRINCIPAUX POINTS DE VENTE DES PUBLICATIONS DE L'OCDE

ARGENTINA – ARGENTINE
Carlos Hirsch S.R.L.
Galería Güemes, Florida 165, 4° Piso
1333 Buenos Aires   Tel. (1) 331.1787 y 331.2391
                     Telefax: (1) 331.1787

AUSTRALIA – AUSTRALIE
D.A. Information Services
648 Whitehorse Road, P.O.B 163
Mitcham, Victoria 3132   Tel. (03) 873.4411
                          Telefax: (03) 873.5679

AUSTRIA – AUTRICHE
Gerold & Co.
Graben 31
Wien I   Tel. (0222) 533.50.14

BELGIUM – BELGIQUE
Jean De Lannoy
Avenue du Roi 202
B-1060 Bruxelles   Tel. (02) 538.51.69/538.08.41
                    Telefax: (02) 538.08.41

CANADA
Renouf Publishing Company Ltd.
1294 Algoma Road
Ottawa, ON K1B 3W8   Tel. (613) 741.4333
                      Telefax: (613) 741.5439
Stores:
61 Sparks Street
Ottawa, ON K1P 5R1   Tel. (613) 238.8985
211 Yonge Street
Toronto, ON M5B 1M4   Tel. (416) 363.3171
                       Telefax: (416)363.59.63

Les Éditions La Liberté Inc.
3020 Chemin Sainte-Foy
Sainte-Foy, PQ G1X 3V6   Tel. (418) 658.3763
                          Telefax: (418) 658.3763

Federal Publications Inc.
165 University Avenue, Suite 701
Toronto, ON M5H 3B8   Tel. (416) 860.1611
                       Telefax: (416) 860.1608

Les Publications Fédérales
1185 Université
Montréal, QC H3B 3A7   Tel. (514) 954.1633
                        Telefax : (514) 954.1635

CHINA – CHINE
China National Publications Import
Export Corporation (CNPIEC)
16 Gongti E. Road, Chaoyang District
P.O. Box 88 or 50
Beijing 100704 PR   Tel. (01) 506.6688
                     Telefax: (01) 506.3101

DENMARK – DANEMARK
Munksgaard Book and Subscription Service
35, Nørre Søgade, P.O. Box 2148
DK-1016 København K   Tel. (33) 12.85.70
                       Telefax: (33) 12.93.87

FINLAND – FINLANDE
Akateeminen Kirjakauppa
Keskuskatu 1, P.O. Box 128
00100 Helsinki

Subscription Services/Agence d'abonnements :
P.O. Box 23
00371 Helsinki   Tel. (358 0) 12141
                  Telefax: (358 0) 121.4450

FRANCE
OECD/OCDE
Mail Orders/Commandes par correspondance:
2, rue André-Pascal
75775 Paris Cedex 16   Tel. (33-1) 45.24.82.00
                        Telefax: (33-1) 49.10.42.76
                        Telex: 640048 OCDE

OECD Bookshop/Librairie de l'OCDE :
33, rue Octave-Feuillet
75016 Paris   Tel. (33-1) 45.24.81.67
               (33-1) 45.24.81.81

Documentation Française
29, quai Voltaire
75007 Paris   Tel. 40.15.70.00

Gibert Jeune (Droit-Économie)
6, place Saint-Michel
75006 Paris   Tel. 43.25.91.19

Librairie du Commerce International
10, avenue d'Iéna
75016 Paris   Tel. 40.73.34.60

Librairie Dunod
Université Paris-Dauphine
Place du Maréchal de Lattre de Tassigny
75016 Paris   Tel. (1) 44.05.40.13

Librairie Lavoisier
11, rue Lavoisier
75008 Paris   Tel. 42.65.39.95

Librairie L.G.D.J. - Montchrestien
20, rue Soufflot
75005 Paris   Tel. 46.33.89.85

Librairie des Sciences Politiques
30, rue Saint-Guillaume
75007 Paris   Tel. 45.48.36.02

P.U.F.
49, boulevard Saint-Michel
75005 Paris   Tel. 43.25.83.40

Librairie de l'Université
12a, rue Nazareth
13100 Aix-en-Provence   Tel. (16) 42.26.18.08

Documentation Française
165, rue Garibaldi
69003 Lyon   Tel. (16) 78.63.32.23

Librairie Decitre
29, place Bellecour
69002 Lyon   Tel. (16) 72.40.54.54

GERMANY – ALLEMAGNE
OECD Publications and Information Centre
August-Bebel-Allee 6
D-53175 Bonn 2   Tel. (0228) 959.120
                  Telefax: (0228) 959.12.17

GREECE – GRÈCE
Librairie Kauffmann
Mavrokordatou 9
106 78 Athens   Tel. (01) 32.55.321
                 Telefax: (01) 36.33.967

HONG-KONG
Swindon Book Co. Ltd.
13–15 Lock Road
Kowloon, Hong Kong   Tel. 366.80.31
                      Telefax: 739.49.75

HUNGARY – HONGRIE
Euro Info Service
POB 1271
1464 Budapest   Tel. (1) 111.62.16
                 Telefax : (1) 111.60.61

ICELAND – ISLANDE
Mál Mog Menning
Laugavegi 18, Pósthólf 392
121 Reykjavik   Tel. 162.35.23

INDIA – INDE
Oxford Book and Stationery Co.
Scindia House
New Delhi 110001   Tel.(11) 331.5896/5308
                    Telefax: (11) 332.5993

17 Park Street
Calcutta 700016   Tel. 240832

INDONESIA – INDONÉSIE
Pdii-Lipi
P.O. Box 269/JKSMG/88
Jakarta 12790   Tel. 583467
                 Telex: 62 875

IRELAND – IRLANDE
TDC Publishers – Library Suppliers
12 North Frederick Street
Dublin 1   Tel. (01) 874.48.35
            Telefax: (01) 874.84.16

ISRAEL
Electronic Publications only
Publications électroniques seulement
Praedicta
5 Shatna Street
P.O. Box 34030
Jerusalem 91340   Tel. (2) 52.84.90/1/2
                   Telefax: (2) 52.84.93

ITALY – ITALIE
Libreria Commissionaria Sansoni
Via Duca di Calabria 1/1
50125 Firenze   Tel. (055) 64.54.15
                 Telefax: (055) 64.12.57
Via Bartolini 29
20155 Milano   Tel. (02) 36.50.83

Editrice e Libreria Herder
Piazza Montecitorio 120
00186 Roma   Tel. 679.46.28
              Telefax: 678.47.51

Libreria Hoepli
Via Hoepli 5
20121 Milano   Tel. (02) 86.54.46
                Telefax: (02) 805.28.86

Libreria Scientifica
Dott. Lucio de Biasio 'Aeiou'
Via Coronelli, 6
20146 Milano   Tel. (02) 48.95.45.52
                Telefax: (02) 48.95.45.48

JAPAN – JAPON
OECD Publications and Information Centre
Landic Akasaka Building
2-3-4 Akasaka, Minato-ku
Tokyo 107   Tel. (81.3) 3586.2016
             Telefax: (81.3) 3584.7929

KOREA – CORÉE
Kyobo Book Centre Co. Ltd.
P.O. Box 1658, Kwang Hwa Moon
Seoul   Tel. 730.78.91
         Telefax: 735.00.30

MALAYSIA – MALAISIE
Co-operative Bookshop Ltd.
University of Malaya
P.O. Box 1127, Jalan Pantai Baru
59700 Kuala Lumpur
Malaysia   Tel. 756.5000/756.5425
            Telefax: 757.3661

MEXICO – MEXIQUE
Revistas y Periodicos Internacionales S.A. de C.V
Florencia 57 - 1004
Mexico, D.F. 06600   Tel. 207.81.00
                      Telefax : 208.39.79

NETHERLANDS – PAYS-BAS
SDU Uitgeverij Plantijnstraat
Externe Fondsen
Postbus 20014
2500 EA's-Gravenhage   Tel. (070) 37.89.880
Voor bestellingen: Telefax: (070) 34.75.778

**NEW ZEALAND
NOUVELLE-ZÉLANDE**
Legislation Services
P.O. Box 12418
Thorndon, Wellington Tel. (04) 496.5652
Telefax: (04) 496.5698

NORWAY – NORVÈGE
Narvesen Info Center – NIC
Bertrand Narvesens vei 2
P.O. Box 6125 Etterstad
0602 Oslo 6 Tel. (022) 57.33.00
Telefax: (022) 68.19.01

PAKISTAN
Mirza Book Agency
65 Shahrah Quaid-E-Azam
Lahore 54000 Tel. (42) 353.601
Telefax: (42) 231.730

PHILIPPINE – PHILIPPINES
International Book Center
5th Floor, Filipinas Life Bldg.
Ayala Avenue
Metro Manila Tel. 81.96.76
Telex 23312 RHP PH

PORTUGAL
Livraria Portugal
Rua do Carmo 70-74
Apart. 2681
1200 Lisboa Tel.: (01) 347.49.82/5
Telefax: (01) 347.02.64

SINGAPORE – SINGAPOUR
Gower Asia Pacific Pte Ltd.
Golden Wheel Building
41, Kallang Pudding Road, No. 04-03
Singapore 1334 Tel. 741.5166
Telefax: 742.9356

SPAIN – ESPAGNE
Mundi-Prensa Libros S.A.
Castelló 37, Apartado 1223
Madrid 28001 Tel. (91) 431.33.99
Telefax: (91) 575.39.98

Libreria Internacional AEDOS
Consejo de Ciento 391
08009 – Barcelona Tel. (93) 488.30.09
Telefax: (93) 487.76.59

Llibreria de la Generalitat
Palau Moja
Rambla dels Estudis, 118
08002 – Barcelona
(Subscripcions) Tel. (93) 318.80.12
(Publicacions) Tel. (93) 302.67.23
Telefax: (93) 412.18.54

SRI LANKA
Centre for Policy Research
c/o Colombo Agencies Ltd.
No. 300-304, Galle Road
Colombo 3 Tel. (1) 574240, 573551-2
Telefax: (1) 575394, 510711

SWEDEN – SUÈDE
Fritzes Information Center
Box 16356
Regeringsgatan 12
106 47 Stockholm Tel. (08) 690.90.90
Telefax: (08) 20.50.21

Subscription Agency/Agence d'abonnements :
Wennergren-Williams Info AB
P.O. Box 1305
171 25 Solna Tel. (08) 705.97.50
Téléfax : (08) 27.00.71

SWITZERLAND – SUISSE
Maditec S.A. (Books and Periodicals - Livres
et périodiques)
Chemin des Palettes 4
Case postale 266
1020 Renens Tel. (021) 635.08.65
Telefax: (021) 635.07.80

Librairie Payot S.A.
4, place Pépinet
CP 3212
1002 Lausanne Tel. (021) 341.33.48
Telefax: (021) 341.33.45

Librairie Unilivres
6, rue de Candolle
1205 Genève Tel. (022) 320.26.23
Telefax: (022) 329.73.18

Subscription Agency/Agence d'abonnements :
Dynapresse Marketing S.A.
38 avenue Vibert
1227 Carouge Tel. (022) 308.07.89
Telefax : (022) 308.07.99

See also – Voir aussi :
OECD Publications and Information Centre
August-Bebel-Allee 6
D-53175 Bonn 2 (Germany) Tel. (0228) 959.120
Telefax: (0228) 959.12.17

TAIWAN – FORMOSE
Good Faith Worldwide Int'l. Co. Ltd.
9th Floor, No. 118, Sec. 2
Chung Hsiao E. Road
Taipei Tel. (02) 391.7396/391.7397
Telefax: (02) 394.9176

THAILAND – THAÏLANDE
Suksit Siam Co. Ltd.
113, 115 Fuang Nakhon Rd.
Opp. Wat Rajbopith
Bangkok 10200 Tel. (662) 225.9531/2
Telefax: (662) 222.5188

TURKEY – TURQUIE
Kültür Yayinlari Is-Türk Ltd. Sti.
Atatürk Bulvari No. 191/Kat 13
Kavaklidere/Ankara Tel. 428.11.40 Ext. 2458
Dolmabahce Cad. No. 29
Besiktas/Istanbul Tel. 260.71.88
Telex: 43482B

UNITED KINGDOM – ROYAUME-UNI
HMSO
Gen. enquiries Tel. (071) 873 0011
Postal orders only:
P.O. Box 276, London SW8 5DT
Personal Callers HMSO Bookshop
49 High Holborn, London WC1V 6HB
Telefax: (071) 873 8200
Branches at: Belfast, Birmingham, Bristol, Edinburgh, Manchester

UNITED STATES – ÉTATS-UNIS
OECD Publications and Information Centre
2001 L Street N.W., Suite 700
Washington, D.C. 20036-4910 Tel. (202) 785.6323
Telefax: (202) 785.0350

VENEZUELA
Libreria del Este
Avda F. Miranda 52, Aptdo. 60337
Edificio Galipán
Caracas 106 Tel. 951.1705/951.2307/951.1297
Telegram: Libreste Caracas

Subscription to OECD periodicals may also be placed through main subscription agencies.

Les abonnements aux publications périodiques de l'OCDE peuvent être souscrits auprès des principales agences d'abonnement.

Orders and inquiries from countries where Distributors have not yet been appointed should be sent to: OECD Publications Service, 2 rue André-Pascal, 75775 Paris Cedex 16, France.

Les commandes provenant de pays où l'OCDE n'a pas encore désigné de distributeur devraient être adressées à : OCDE, Service des Publications, 2, rue André-Pascal, 75775 Paris Cedex 16, France.

3-1994

OECD PUBLICATIONS, 2 rue André-Pascal, 75775 PARIS CEDEX 16
PRINTED IN FRANCE
(96 94 03 1) ISBN 92-64-14087-5 – No. 47115 1994